THE DREAM DICTIONARY

THE DREAM DICTIONARY

for the Modern Dreamer

Tim Etchells

Duck Editions

First published in 2001 by
Duckworth Literary Entertainments, Ltd.
61 Frith Street, London W1D 3JL
Tel: 020 7434 4242
Fax: 020 7434 4420
email:DuckEd@duckworth-publishers.co.uk
www.ducknet.co.uk

A CIP catalogue record for this book is available
from the British Library

ISBN 0 7156 3108 X

Typeset by Ray Davies
Printed in Great Britain by
Bookcraft (Bath) Ltd, Midsomer Norton, Somerset

For Mark

Acknowledgements

Thanks to my friends, both close and distant in geography for support, advice and vodka. Thanks to my editor Sarah Such for her trust in the idea and to her and the team at Duckworth for their hard work in steering it through.

Introduction

As darkness falls, so begins what some have called the 'cinema of sleep', that flickering shimmer of fragments which plays in loops through the skulls, hearts and eyelids beneath the sheets and blankets of the earth.

There are those who maintain that a dream is not more than the lost, deluded workings in a mind deprived of consciousness and ordering sense. There are those who say that dreams are but figments of an echo of a shadow of a thought. And yet ever since the start of time itself, man [sic] has experienced the wonder and amazement of dreams, and ever since the first savage awoke with puzzlement and the rubbing of eyes people have ventured to interpret the histories, half-stories and feelings unfolded therein.

What secrets does the dreaming mind reveal and how best and most correctly to unlock them? Man has seen his dreams as warnings, as predictions, auguries and omens, he has seen them as clues to the future, to the outcome of love trysts, domestic strife and commercial dilemmas, as fuel for the solution to money troubles and brutal battles, as communications from God, gods and eternal forces of all shapes, dimensions and kinds. As times change and man's wisdom grows there may be disagreements about the modes and types of interpretation – but from the soothsayers, witches and shamans of old to the psychiatrists, pop psychologists and bespectacled dream scientists of the present day we can be sure that all those of discernment and intelligence are agreed on three essential facts: that dreams are important, that we are driven completely insane when deprived of them and that a close and careful interpretation of their contents can unlock the secrets of our sufferings and destinies.

Since writing began in Ancient Egypt there have been a great many big books, and small ones, devoted to the topic of dreams, in all the eras and all the languages of the world. The author of this work is proud to take his place amongst them. The book is focused on Modern Dreams alone, for the twin gods of progress and invention have filled our times with a chaos of new objects, experiences and archetypes, each of which has a hidden symbolic meaning that until now, and the appearance of this volume, has remained in the shadows of darkness and obscurity. While the copious dream books and dictionaries published over many ages have concentrated on those archetypal features of human existence felt to be timeless or universal (chairs, tables, fire, love and falling), the work which you hold in your hands is the first ever devoted to explaining the particular, the transitory and the specifically contemporary as it may appear in the world of our dreams. I hope it serves the reader well.

I must end, sadly, with regrets and with apology, for whilst this venture is forged in the fires of ambition to know and to explicate the landscape of Modern Dreams it is also doomed to an endless and humble failure. The author knows (as must we all) that just as men toil each day to better, change and transform their world there comes each night a new tide, an endless wave of new dreams involving new objects, items, things and situations never felt before. I have done my best to meet this tide, to ride upon it, to make sense of its eddies, its currents and the flotsam which is borne upon it. The rest we must leave to our children.

The Author.
Sheffield, England.
2001.

A

Accused by a Neon Sign

Common is the modern dream that a neon sign has been erected opposite one's house, making a number of serious and damaging accusations.

If the accusations are **true** the dream bodes well.

If they are **false** it bodes ill.

A sign which **blinks on and off, or which contains a humorous pictorial element,** is especially significant.

Acid   *See* **L.S.D.**

Action Replay

To dream of action replayed from a **sporting contest** has no deep significance in a dream, unless it involves a dubious penalty, disputed match point or bitter allegations of tripping, pushing, punching, or other foul play.

In such dreams the meaning lies not in the acrimonious content but in the number of times the particular incident is replayed. **Once** stands for fortune, **twice** for betrayal, **three times** for suspicion and **four times (or more)** for shame and defeat.

A dream of an action replay in which **players are taking deliberate dives, play-acting and hamming up their alleged injuries,** predicts insincerity at home and abroad.

Of greater significance are those well-known Modern Dreams in which **events from the dreamer's own private life are played and played again as action replay.** In such cases close attention must be played to all details, since a dream which features **changes in some subtle aspect of the event** (the colour of a shirt, the gesture of a spouse, the

11

vocal expression of a friend) foretells hard-won progress in a boring, necessary task. If the event replayed is **identical in all aspects to its original occurrence** the dream signifies uncomfortable stasis, a future founded on compromise. If the action replay is in **slow motion, or, worse still, viewed from another angle,** a death by drowning or poisoning is predicted.

Aerosmith   To dream of the rock band Aerosmith foretells that you will have sex with someone who is quite young.

Aerosol   Lightheartedness and a playful spirit will help you through the weeks ahead.

A.I.D.S.   A break with the past.

Air Brakes   Sufferings caused by the ignorance of others.

Air Conditioner   A dream of mixed fortunes.

If **the room is too cold** the future will hold poverty mixed with happiness.

If **the unit is pumping stale air** riches combined with ill-health are in store.

Air Guitar   Doors open, obstacles fall.

Air Jordans   Success by day and by night.

Air Rage   A dream in which one **sits passively through an air rage incident,** terrified as other passengers wreak havoc, singing, throwing bottles and punches, yelling abuse, foretells of promotion, or unexpected respect from one's contemporaries.

To dream that one **takes part in an air rage incident** predicts an encounter with a drunken ex-boyfriend or girlfriend or a child that needs discipline.

If one is cast in the role of a **steward, stewardess or pilot, enduring the aggravation, taunts and physical attacks of passengers,** the dream foretells of a test of strength or patience when dealing with a lover.

12

Air Rifle A dream of an air rifle predicts a minor argument or spat between siblings or family members.

To dream of **shooting at pigeons, starlings, sparrows, cats or dogs with an air rifle** predicts trouble with the law.

Airline Safety Drill The dream concerns the sex life or libido of the dreamer.

If **the steward or stewardess is looking bored or making camp ironic gestures as they plod through the routine** (emergency exits, life jackets and oxygen masks that fall) the dream foretells of a period of sexual excitement, experiment and great satisfaction.

If the cabin staff are **giggling and whispering or making private jokes throughout the dream** it denotes chastity, or sex comprising half-pleasure or impotence.

Airport Novel An airport novel stands for new love from an unexpected quarter.

If the novel is **battered and well-thumbed or water-damaged** the love will not last.

If it has **shiny or embossed lettering on the cover** the love will leave a dent in the dreamer's finances.

To dream of an airport novel with a **cover that features excessive cleavage, gold, guns, diamonds, stockinged legs, high heels, figures in silhouette, lipstick lips or wide-open eyes** is of only minor significance, foretelling as it does of a gift of a painting, ornament or clothing accessory.

AK47 The popular machine-rifle is a symbol of sexual prowess when seen in a dream.

Alcohol-Free Lager Chastisement, compromise, the appearance of contentment.

Alcoholics Anonymous

To dream that you attend a meeting of Alcoholics Anonymous predicts a party or other celebration.

If there are **people weeping** at the AA meeting you should not go to the party.

Alone in the Office at Night

The dreamer works later than any colleague. The sky darkens, the clatter of keyboards and ambient chatter dies and soon gives way to silence. The large windows give clear views of the city with its lights spread out in the darkness below.

If a phone rings on a colleague's desk the dream foretells the arrival of new baby.

If the lift makes a ping-sound to signal an arrival but when the doors open the carriage is vacant the dream is a warning of deception or subterfuge afoot.

A common dream of unhappiness is that of staying late and alone in an office at night as water drips from the suspended ceiling, making its way through the cracks at the edges of the polystyrene roof tiles and down onto the dreamer's desk. The more water there is flooding from the ceiling the more profound the unhappiness will be.

If the dream involves the dreamer waiting for co-workers to leave the building and then removing his or her clothes and sitting at a neighbouring desk the dream predicts a revelation, a chance meeting or a long journey undertaken alone.

Alphabetti Spaghetti

Frequent are the Modern Dreams in which Alphabetti Spaghetti plays a crucial or significant role.

Most common is the dream in which the letters slither from the can in their lurid orange sauce and directly form a sentence in the bottom of the pan. This dream is a reminder to trust one's heart or intuition, and the words spelled out by the spaghetti in this instance are relatively insignificant.

A second common dream is that one's dining companions are conspiring to arrange the letters of one's edible alphabet in surreptitious messages. If the message-maker is one's mother or father, the dream suggests a harmonious Christmas. If the

14

message-maker is a **sibling** or **friend** it suggests a harmonious New Year. **If a stranger spells a message** in the letters of one's Alphabetti Spaghetti it predicts unexpected bills or tax demands.

If the words **FORGER, FORGET, FOREVER** or **FUTURE** appear written out in the letters of the playfully shaped pasta, then future plans with which one has struggled for some time should finally and unequivocally be cancelled.

Aluminium Ladder

A dream of an aluminium ladder signifies rapid promotion at work. If the ladder **appears to have no beginning and no conceivable end** the promotion will be considerable but subject to impulsive reversal.

Amusement Arcade

See **Games Arcade**

Animal Hospital

To find yourself in the **waiting room** of an animal hospital indicates an appointment you have no wish to keep. The bigger the cage you are clutching the more unpleasant the forthcoming appointment.

If **hideous sounds are emerging from the consulting room** the dream betokens a victory in a contest, competition or game of chance.

Animal Testing

See **Lab Rats**

Animals

Many and diverse are the uniquely Modern Dreams involving animals, which, running wild in the complex landscapes of the contemporary world, provide a range of rich and powerful symbols in the cinema of sleep.

First we shall consider the common dreams of **animals caught or entrapped in some especially Modern circumstance,** the most frequently occurring of which is that of **a horse tangled in barbed wire; the more it struggles the more it strangles itself.** This dream predicts an unhappy marriage or business partnership; or a rich collaboration in the field of music. If **the horse dies**

15

you will suffer unhappiness at the hands of another.

Common also is the dream of a **poodle in a microwave**. If **the poodle is calm as the microwave bombardment begins** you will face unexpected adversity with resilience and strength. If **the poodle panics** you will be visited by ghosts, unwelcome relatives or bad memories.

By contrast the dreams of **a hamster trapped in a tumble dryer** and that of **a cat entombed in ice inside a deep freeze** are good dreams predicting the giddy heights of happiness and the solid strengths of friendship respectively.

Beyond such dreams of animals caught or entrapped there are the dreams of **animals which appear only fleetingly in specific Modern settings**. A dream of **a dog which appears mysteriously on some patch of urban wasteground** foretells change predicated on the late arrival of a letter; whilst to glimpse **a cat sunning itself on the shelves in the window of a supermarket** predicts worldly pleasure.

See also **Birds Sitting on Telephone Wires** *and* **Cat with Fireworks Tied to its Tail**

Anthrax

A debate or disagreement will be solved by tact, a secret will be uncovered by accident.

Anti-Dandruff Shampoo

There is no meaning for anti-dandruff shampoo when it first appears in a dream, but if it **recurs** the dream is one of love lost and then found again.

Appearing in Blackface Make-up at the Truth Commission

The dream is of no great significance, predicting an argument with neighbours or a social embarrassment of a common kind.

Arm Trapped between the Central Heating Pipes

The dreamer (most frequently cast in the role of a child) reaches between the pipes to retrieve a pencil or some other valued object. In pushing the hand

16

further, or in twisting the arm, straining at some preposterous angle to reach the item in question the dreamer becomes trapped. The pipes, warm at the start of the adventure, are in the process of growing hotter. The dreamer calls for help.

If **help comes** the dream foresees travel.

If **help does not come** the dream foretells that the dreamer's life has reached a physical, emotional and intellectual plateau.

If the dreamer **becomes surrounded by other children who are distressed and weeping** the dream predicts a breakdown in a family or business relationship.

Army Surplus Clothing

Economies forced by necessity, pleasures truncated by force.

Artificial Beach

To dream of an artificial beach composed of smooth white sand in gentle rolling dunes predicts a time of harmony and relaxation.

If the beach dreamed of is **beside an artificial ocean/lake**, its waves created by some complex machinery hidden in the depths, the meaning of the dream is reversed, signalling as it does a time of unease and troubled thoughts concerning people or plans that are important to you.

To dream of an artificial beach **contained in a holiday resort inside a geodesic dome**, a temperate **micro-climate baking its sand to delicious perfection** augurs ill for those with business, sporting or culinary ambitions.

Artificial Heart

Honesty, truth.

Artificial Limbs

The dreamer will suffer a fraud.

If the limbs have a **realistic texture and skin-colouring** the dream signifies dishonesty in a friend and deception in a colleague.

If the limbs have **complex internal hydraulics and electronics** the dreamer will perpetrate a crime.

17

Artist-in-Residence

Subterfuge and dissembling, delirium from fever or from alcohol.

If the artist has **a beard** you will be swept way with happiness.

Asbestos Something nasty will come out of your roof.

Asbestos Suit You are frightened of the future.

Asian Corner Shop

A dream of an Asian corner shop that **sells everything from toothpaste to colouring books, fish-food, sellotape, plugboards and newspapers,** predicts disputes over boundaries and territory, and domestic arguments concerning rentals and ownership.

If there are **loads of Asian kids hanging around behind the counter** you will be blessed with good luck.

If **the door is open behind the counter and you can see through to the front room and what they are watching on the TV** you will encounter unexpected hardships by night.

Assembly Line The industrial assembly line, with its repetitive, degrading working conditions and its trance-inducing boredom is a common setting for many Modern Dreams.

If **work continues unabated** the dream bodes well.

If the **routine is disrupted by laughter, pranks or even conversation** the dream bodes ill.

If **the pace of work on the assembly line keeps increasing, forcing the dreamer to a delirium of faster and faster movements,** the dream predicts the onslaught of an exercise fad.

Asset Stripping You will be rich but hated and feared rather than loved.

Astrophysics A dream of regret. Events buried deep in the past remain haunting, problematic and unsolved. A common dream is that in which observed glitches in the orbits and rotation of visible bodies in the heavens give rise to the assumed existence, position and size of a newcomer. This dream of **the discovery of new stellar object by calculation alone** foretells of harm caused by suspicion or guilt caused by gossip.

Atoms

A dream of atoms predicts the loss of an argument, confusion over the parentage of a child or a legal search to determine ownership of a house, land or other property.

If **the atoms are spinning rapidly in a seeming-eternity of microscopic space**, the dream foretells of a crisis in matters financial.

Audio Tape Tangled in the Branches of a Tree

The branches of the trees on the boulevards of many Modern Dreams are replete with these shiny brown decorations, remnants of smashed cassette tapes, the tangles and streamers of the tape blowing in the wind.

If the tape **threatens to strangle the tree**, blocking it from the light or binding its spindly branches tightly, the dream wans of a danger from forces you had previously thought weak.

If the tape **brushes your face** like some electromagnetic spider's web, or **becomes entangled in your hair**, the dream predicts a mystery encounter with a stranger on a bus or boat or on a visit to a graveyard.

In one classic example of Modern Dreaming the **wind blows through the cassette tape as it flutters,** caught high in the branches of some oak, elm or ash, **causing the music on the tape itself to play.** If you hear **light classical music** you will soon have a rise in pay; if you hear **pub rock, pomp rock** or **punk rock** you will meet a man with bad debts of whom you should beware.

Finally, if the tape entrapped in the branches **emits the sound of a children's song or recorded**

19

story, the voice of the adult narrator echoing and calling out amongst the falling leaves, then the dream foretells of a journey to a place that means a lot to you – a place where you grew up, spent holidays in your youth, or where you enjoyed an adult romance.

See also **Tape Jammed or Tangled** *and* **Ghost Message on the Answering Machine**

Audio Tour

To dream that the audio tour of a museum, gallery or public building is misleading, fictitious or factually incorrect foretells of the resurrection of a longstanding argument, a promise broken or a sharp exchange of words with a spouse, parent or grandparent.

If the tour is in a foreign language or if low batteries make the otherwise upbeat and informative commentary sound like desperate wails from the undead the dream predicts problems with borders, peripheries and travel plans.

If the audio tour concerns itself with the landscape of your hitherto private life – a commentary on your old school playgrounds or on the diverse bedrooms in which you have slept throughout your life – the dream bodes ill in each possible aspect.

Automatic Doors

A symbol of progress (or lack of it) towards one's goals. Operated by infra-red or pressure pads, the common type of Modern door which greets one's approach by opening wide with a mechanical hiss, relates especially to success or failure in the sphere of careers and employment.

The potent dream that automatic doors will not open for you indicates a great change in status. For the already powerful this dream of exclusion and humiliation before a great public building foretells of a demise. For those less fortunate the dream may foretell of a change of luck.

Automaton

A dream of honesty, strength of spirit, confidence in love.

B

Baby Seat

To dream of a baby's moulded plastic car seat foresees a misunderstanding with a close friend.

If **the seat covering is tartan** you will be free from worries.

A dream in which **you have placed the baby in the car seat on the roof of the car and then forgotten about it and driven away** is a warning of losses in love, debts in business and despair in the heart.

Backing Singers are More Beautiful than You are

The dreamer is singing in a top spot in a Christmas TV special and, as the song lumbers on, is faced with a growing realisation that the cameras are concentrating on the three brunette backing singers, in identical if skimpy outfits, standing behind. The dream is one of its opposite – the insecurity it pantomimes will be felt as confidence and success in real life.

If the backing singers are wearing **red leather or black PVC** the dream is a warning that unchecked passions may get the dreamer into trouble.

If the backing singers are **muscular men in black g-strings** the dream foretells of a change in the dreamer's sexual orientation.

Back-Projection

A dream which features back-projection predicts feelings of alienation. The more obvious the back-projection the worse the feelings will be.

If the back-projection is that of **the streets of a city as seen from the back window of a car** you will travel far, whilst a dream of a back-projected view **from a train** foretells that someone will try to do you harm.

21

Bad Thing Somewhere in the House

A Modern Fear dream in which there is an amorphous and unnameable bad thing somewhere in the house. In these disquieting contemporary scenarios of sleep, danger is ever present but its source remains unknowable or at best ill-defined, the unease living in the dreamer or dispersed across some landscape, atmosphere or set of diverse objects.

The dream of a bad thing will often focus on some special part or feature of a house – on the **stairwell**, on the **doors to certain rooms**, on the **image or texture of a wallpaper** or on the **shadowy interiors of cupboards or closets** but what the bad thing is, its form or purpose, is never revealed. In fact, for the most part, the dream of a bad thing depends for its meaning on the temperature in the house. A **cold** house indicates future prosperity, whilst a **warm** or **hot** house indicates a future of impoverished misery.

See also **Modern Fear**

Balkanisation of Domestic Space

A dream in which one's house, apartment or bed-sit is divided into separate areas or republics due to a domestic dispute is generally considered a sign of good luck.

The **creation of blockades using furniture**, the **conversion of rooms into refugee or holding camps**, and the **introduction of rotas for cleaning and shopping duties** often form a part of such dreams, whose correct interpretation is based on the opportunity such strife may provide for the re-organisation of one's life.

Ball Room

Since a ballroom for dancing in is not truly Modern and therefore beyond the stated province of this dictionary, readers who have dreamed of dancing are directed to the entries **Breakdancing, Discothèque** *and* **Foam Party.**

Of concern to us here is that type of ball room

commonly found at a motorway services or dedicated kids' play zone – a large glass-walled room filled almost to bursting with coloured plastic balls and screaming, fighting children. The dream predicts a change of career.

To **stand outside and plot the complex vectors of the children and the tumbling balls** predicts a new job in physics, maths or engineering.

To dream of **entering the ball pool, diving deep into its chaos and danger,** predicts a job in Hollywood, the film business or corporate finance.

Bangles Reform   The Bangles are a symbol of musical difficulties. The dreamer must avoid professional singing at all costs, although karaoke and pub-sing-along may be attempted without harm.

See also **Beatles Reform** *and* **Led Zeppelin Reunion**

Barbecue made with Road-Kill

This dream of unsavoury sustenance is common and has no deep meaning.

If the barbecue is **domestic cat or dog** it can suggest that a surprise holiday is on the cards.

If the barbecue includes **hedgehog, weasel** or **racoon** the holiday should best be avoided.

Barbie Fights   To dream of a fight between two Barbie dolls is a warning of a conflict of interest at work or a personal problem of conscience for the dreamer, especially if the dolls are **billed as Good Barbie vs. Bad Barbie and dressed up accordingly in flowing pastels and tight black or red.**

If **Good Barbie wins** the fight you will find a satisfying solution to the dilemma at hand, whilst if the **leather-clad Bad Barbie wins** your conscience will find no way through.

A dream of **Barbie dolls fighting in a muddy puddle or in a washing-up bowl filled with foam or jelly** foretells of war; or sanctions, brinkmanship and months of hopeless propaganda skirmishes.

Baseball Cap   A dream of success for a friend or family member. If the cap is **worn backwards** the dream predicts reversal of fortunes.

Bathing in Diet Lilt

A veneer of happiness will cover your emptiness endlessly.

See also **Chicken Cooked in Tango, Cut Your Finger and Pepsi Comes Out** *and* **Diet Pepsi.**

Bathroom Suite made of Gold

You will be unhappy.

Batman   Secrecy, honour, resilience, strength.

Battle of Seattle/Prague

You have watchful enemies who seek to injure your business.

See also **Tear Gas**

Beatles Reform   The Beatles were the original Fab Four from Liverpool, England. To dream of them when pregnant means you will have quads. To dream of them in other circumstances tells you to focus on the lucky number four in any lottery, bingo or other game of chance.

See also **Bangles Reform** *and* **Led Zeppelin Reunion**

Beatniks   To dream of Beatniks predicts amazement and wonder.

Bedrooms, Kitchen, Stairwell and Living Rooms of the House are Littered with Discarded Packaging in Ambiguous Shapes formed from Moulded Polystyrene

This uniquely Modern form of detritus is a symbol of an untidy mind, of a dreamer who is bothered by many projects, plans, desires and problems all in some state of incompletion. The larger the polystyrene forms dreamed as they litter the landscape of the house the more likely it is that the problems may be solved.

If the forms are **broken, dented** or **smashed** the problems will be made worse by the efforts of others, who are only trying to help.

If the polystyrene shapes **have forms reminiscent of persons, beasts** or **aspects of a cityscape** the dreamer will be hampered by memories, forced to abandon projects or to travel far in the company of a stranger.

The meaning of the dream and its predictions for solutions may be most precisely defined by noting the location of the discarded packaging. If it is **clustered in the bedroom** sex or romance could solve the dreamer's ills, if it is clustered **in the kitchen** the solution could be cleanliness or cookery and so on.

Berlin Wall	Divisions in the family, a crisis of conscience, luck in a context of hardship.

To dream that one is **chipping pieces from the Berlin Wall** portends a future of poverty and cynicism.

Bike Courier	A dream of a bike courier predicts the loss or death of a friend.
Billboard	If the billboard shows **a face with an enigmatic smile** you will be happy, whilst if it shows a **country landscape, desert** or **sunny beach** you will leave your current abode and move on to pastures new.

To dream of a billboard which features a **complex linguistic pun** or a **near-incomprehensible visual gag** foretells that you will struggle with homework, assessments or tests.

To dream of **defacing a billboard** foretells illness; if **words are written or obscured** the illness will be of the mouth or the tongue, whilst if **human figures on a billboard are defaced** (eyes erased, genitals scratched, breasts sprayed), the illness will mirror exactly these sites of damage to the billboard.

See also **Accused by a Neon Sign**

Bin Liners Full of Clothes left in the Doorway of a Charity Shop
The dream warns against abandoning plans too soon, against losing direction and against the frailties of memory.

Binoculars
If used at a sporting event, opera or in a wildlife reserve, binoculars foretell of an opportunity arising that should be valued and taken.

If used improperly – to spy on strangers or on a lover – binoculars stand for the discovery of an unpleasant or unfortunate secret.

Biological Detergent
Unknown enemies, unexpected phone calls, blood feuds or arguments.

Biological Father
To dream of your biological father foretells of a time of carefree success, whilst a dream of your **biological mother** dream foretells of a time of doubt and disillusionment.

Biological Warfare
Travel in the company of friends, sleepless nights in the company of strangers.

Birds Sitting on Telephone Wires
Someone will gain information about you through deception.

See also **Animals** *and* **Cat with Fireworks Tied to its Tail**

Biro has Leaked in your Pocket
If the blue-black substance has worked itself right into the corner of your pocket and stained through the material, becoming visible from the other side, the dream indicates that a secret will be revealed.

Black Market Video
To dream of a video in which the **picture is badly dubbed** or the **sound quality is poor** is to dream of a long, happy life to come, whilst if there are **sections of the film missing** you will suffer blackouts.

A dream of a black market video in which the

26

entire end of the film is missing or erased foretells of a lost job, an unexpected departure by night, or a change of address.

If the bootleg video has evidently been filmed on a handheld camcorder by some bozo sitting in the front row of a cinema, the image wandering in and out of focus, the sound distorting and the whole film marred by occasional gratuitous close-ups of some small part of the screen, as if the person making the video was more interested in the grain of Kate Winslet's eyebrow than anything else the dream foretells of a storm in the ocean of your emotions and the need for a lifeguard to be on duty at all times.

Blasted Off into Space

You will start a great adventure and find it quite dangerous.

Blaxploitation   You will be the unwitting victim of a practical joke or fraud.

Blood Flowing from the Showerhead or Faucet

To dream that blood has replaced water in the taps or shower of your own house foretells of an argument.

To dream that blood flows freely from the taps in a hotel bathroom predicts genocide.

Blood in the Spit in the Toilets

Elegance, beauty, grace and wealth combined.

Blood Test   To take a blood test in a dream indicates that one's family are not trusting or confident in one's abilities.

To pass the test means that one will regain this confidence and trust.

To fail it means continuing doubts and possible expulsion.

Blood Transfusion

To dream that one is lying prone in a hospital bed, pyjama'd and hooked up with tubes for a blood transfusion, denotes weakness in a close or valued relationship. To the newsagent it may mean a pilfering delivery boy, to the gangster an untrustworthy henchman, to the politician a dishonest press secretary.

If the dream of a transfusion goes on for a long time, one's blood draining and draining, calling for a nurse but none coming and the blood filling bottles and bottles and then overflowing, until eventually one starts to black out it predicts good sport in the making of a child.

Blow-out   A dream of a high speed blow-out foretells of a life of drudgery and toil. The more dramatic the blow-out and its consequences in the dream the more dull and predictable one's life will become.

Blue Movies   *See* X-rated Films

Blu-Tack™   You will find new friends.

If the dream is of greasy translucent blu-tack stains marking the walls of a house into which you have moved, the arrangement of the marks providing an archaeology of its previous decoration with posters, postcards and clippings you will come to regret a decision made recently and in haste.

Body Bag   The nights for you will be long and dark.

Bohemians   You will be robbed.

Boil-in-the-Bag Foodstuffs
Nakedness in the eyes of a friend-become-enemy.

Bomb Tests   You will become ill. The illness will concentrate on the area of your heart, liver or lungs.

Bond Girls   For a woman strength, good luck and a chance for self-determination. For a man danger, travel, fear of death.

If the Bond Girls are sleeping the meaning of the dream is reversed.

28

If they are **doing karate** the meaning is multiplied in strength.

Bono	You will meet an Irish man.
Boom Mic	Ears at the window, eyes at the keyhole.
Borstal	Intransigence, slowness, fear at night.
Bouncers	The dream of bouncers in white shirts and black bow-ties is largely a fortuitous one, depending on the time of night at which they are seen.

To dream of bouncers in the **soft glow of early evening when the light has not yet fully gone from the sky** is especially agreeable. If the bouncers are **standing in the doorway of a night-club at this time, laughing pleasantly and practising karate chops, kicks and other cool fight moves,** then the meaning of the dream is strengthened considerably.

A dream of bouncers **at midnight, eyeing up pretty girls and giving their best strong-but-silent nods to blokes as they enter the club** foretells of a chance encounter with a very pleasant outcome.

A dream of bouncers **at 3am, sitting around a table and enjoying a quiet pint and a laugh together after a hard night's work,** augurs well for those in medicine, insurance and the law.

Only in one dream is the association of the bouncer with general good fortune ever broken, namely that in which bouncers are **stamping on someone's stomach and then throwing them headfirst into an unlit stairwell.** This dream foretells of a business failure or a family dispute.

See also **Discothèque**

Bouncy Castle These lurid inflatable palaces, bringing colour and excitement to parks, public gardens and the forecourts and car parks of DIY superstores, with their rubberised turrets and gaily-painted windows, are frequently-appearing symbols of the past.

To dream of **fighting in a bouncy castle** warns the dreamer to expect troubles connected with his or her history in marriage or in romance.

If the dreamer's assailants in the fight are **children** the dream predicts complications following divorce.

To dream of **having sexual intercourse** in a bouncy castle foretells of a visit from the dreamer's latest former lover; whilst to dream of **seeking entry to a bouncy castle but that such entry is denied** suggests divorce for the married and rejection for those who are in love.

Bowie, David
David Bowie, the self-styled chameleon of rock, is a symbol of stasis and frustration in a dream. If Bowie looks **androgynous** you will suffer setbacks at work.

Brain Scan
To dream that one is lying prone on a gurney, being propelled head first into the high-tech drum of a CAT scan machine predicts a time of fun and harmless mischief with a friend.

Braxton, Toni
Toni Braxton is an omen of hope and better times ahead.

Breakdancing
The dream predicts a crisis which the dreamer will survive.

If a **crowd has gathered round** and they are whooping and clapping and blowing whistles, the dreamer's success will be made possible by friends.

If **white people** are breakdancing the dream predicts the loss of something or someone dear to the dreamer.

Breast Implants
A dream of breast implants predicts good luck to come. The precise amount of good fortune is governed by this simple formula: the bigger the implants, the brighter and more positive the future will be.

A dream of breast implants with **faint scars visible** (around the nipples or under the curve of the breasts) predicts that happiness will be bought at a price.

If the implants are **dangerous** (infected, burst) the meaning of the dream is reversed.

See also **Plastic Surgery**

Breath Test

Breath is a traditional symbol for the soul, and the act of testing it in a dream signifies a spiritual challenge or hurdle which must be overcome.

If the **policeman (or woman) who administers the test is courteous and polite** you may overcome your challenges; if he or she is **rude or impatient** you may not, with consequences of hardship and compromise.

If the breath test **takes place at night** it indicates a secret answer to your problems.

Briefcase with a Bomb Inside

There will be an explosion.

Brieze Blocks

A dream of these ubiquitous, light-weight grey-coloured building blocks depends for its meaning on their *arrangement*.

If the brieze blocks are **stacked in a neat cube or cubes**, awaiting use, the dream augurs well for current projects, plans and relationships.

If the brieze blocks are **scattered here and there, strewn on the floor as if following some storm or act of vandalism** the dream is a portent of mental disorder, a warning of bad plans and targets which will not be reached.

A dream of **broken brieze blocks** – snapped in half or crushed and crumbled – denotes a union of marriage or of business ventures.

Bubbles under Lino

Imbalance in a marriage, conflicts and tensions arising from the past.

Bucket of Water on Top of a Door

To dream of this hilarious practical joke indicates success in the construction of theories, scale models, making plans or diagrams.

If the dreamer is **hit by a bucket of water as it**

falls from above he or she will suffer from a setback in the realm of passion or desire.

See also **Custard Pie Fight**

Buffy the Vampire Slayer

A dream of the blonde slayer foretells of a struggle of wills with a lover or with a boss or colleague at work.

If Buffy is **smiling** you will win. If **she frowns or pouts** you will lose.

A dream of **Buffy held captive by demons** predicts romance in an unexpected quarter.

Bullet-Proof Glass Sight and danger combined, threats from water, earth and the air.

Bullet-Proof Vest A dream of a bullet-proof vest **worn under the shirt** stands for secrets and subterfuge.

If the protective vest is **worn openly,** on top of other clothing, the dream stands for danger and for promises broken.

Bum Bag Ingratitude, problems of ethics, morals or lost religious faith.

Bungee Jumping The dream starts at the top of the crane tower, just before descent. The dreamer tips forward and there are long precious seconds of freefall which seem to last forever. When the fall reaches the length of the bungee rope it begins to stretch, getting longer and longer as the dreamer comes perilously close to the ground before rebounding in an upwards direction.

If the bungee jump takes place **in a field at some provincial fête** the dream is a reminder of the importance of family and community.

If it takes place **in the concrete backyard of an urban pub, amongst the empty barrels and other detritus, and is accompanied by drunken exhortations, yells and tomfoolery in the drop zone** the dream is a warning about unsuitable and uncaring acquaintances or friends.

Burning a Library To dream that you are part of a mob burning a library foretells that you will make new friends.

Burst Condom A common Modern Dream which may portend ill health.

Burying White Goods

The dreamer digs a hole at night, at the edge of a golf course, in a wood or in some far-flung portion of a playing field. By torchlight a fridge, deep freeze, microwave or other consumer item is removed from under a blanket in the trunk of a car, dragged into place and then buried in the makeshift grave. The dream is that of impending seduction.

If the white goods are **successfully buried** the dreamer will be seduced.

If they are **half-buried or simply too heavy to move** the seduction will fail.

Bus Driver Constantly Accelerating and Braking and Swearing and Cutting Up Other Drivers and Talking to Himself and Skidding and Changing Lanes as if He is in a Big Emergency to get the Route done and get Back to Base or as if He Thinks He is in Some Kind of Thriller

The dream predicts a holiday in the mountains or by water, an evening of cool and pleasant conversation and a welcome return to a sedentary life.

Buying a VCR from the Boot of a Car

The dreamer finds him or herself in the back yard of a pub, or in the wasteland of some rubble-strewn car park. Prices are discussed and a VCR is produced from the trunk of a car.

If the VCR is **wrapped in a blanket** the dream predicts a birth.

If it is **wrapped in a polythene bag or bin liner** the dream predicts a death.

A hasty and illegal transaction of this kind often occurs as part of a so-called **Daylight Dream** in which **events that belong in the night-time are transposed to broad daylight.**

See also **Daylight Dreams**

33

C

Canned Goods   The dream predicts boredom, loss and repetition.

Canned Laughter   If canned laughter plays for the dreamer **in a public situation** (railway station, restaurant, street) the dream bodes ill.

If it plays **in the privacy of the dreamer's home on some family occasion** (birthday, christening, wake) it is a good omen for future ventures involving travel or music.

If canned laughter **follows the dreamer even when he or she is alone** (in bed, in the shower, whilst driving the car at night) then the dream is ambiguous.

If the laughter comes in **short staccato bursts** it tends to the negative; if it comes in **long, near-constant waves** it tends more towards the positive.

The Modern Dreamer should fear deeply the dream in which a **single taped or 'canned' female voice laughs endlessly in absolute hysteria.** Known to many as the laughing woman dream, or the crazy woman dream, it warns of emotional storms, upset and crisis on the cards.

Cannon Fodder   The dreamer looks at his or her compatriots and knows, in one split second, that they are all cannon fodder; that they will be sacrificed in some battle-to-come; that they will all die.

The meaning of the dream is in the look of realisation – if it is **blank or resigned** there will be a prosperous harvest, if there are **tears in the dreamer's eyes** there will be a hard winter or a terrible storm.

Car Bomb	A dream of a car bomb predicts a change in the weather.
Car Boot Sale	The past will return on you, wreaking vengeance and threatening prosperity, up-ending stability.
Car Broken Into	If the thieves have **smashed the fascia of the dashboard** the dream predicts seven years of bad luck.

If they have **stolen the cassette player** you will soon be at a celebration where you should be most careful of quarrelling.

If the thieves have **slept, defecated or urinated in the car** the dream predicts a change of address.

If the thieves have **bled in the car, leaving sticky dark circular stains on the dark brown upholstery,** the dream warns of a missing child.

Car Chase	Love from an unexpected quarter will greet those who dream of being pursued at high speed in a car chase.

If **the dreamer is the pursuer not the pursued** he or she will face a month of bitterness and trials.

If the car chase **takes place in the beautiful American city of San Francisco, with the cars flying up off the tops of the big hills at high speed and thundering through fog across the stop signs at the bottom** the dream signifies loneliness which may only be solved by travel.

If the **cars go crashing into Chinatown where there just happens to be a Chinese New Year parade, causing the revellers to panic, trashing the dancing dragons etc.,** the meaning of the dream is this: a phone call will be made and a suitcase will be packed, a present will be returned and a letter, once written, will remain forever unsent.

A dream of a car chase **at night** with its abstracts of darkness, double strips of sodium lamps and speeding, flickering lights has its own unique meaning in nature's wonderful cinema of sleep. The dream signifies love and the imminent threat of its death.

A car chase **in the desert** signifies emptiness.
A car chase **in the mountains** signifies grief.

Car Crash

The dream predicts its opposite. You will get a new car or bicycle.

If the car crash in the dream is **especially savage** you may become rich and own a whole fleet of cars.

More common and yet no less significant is the dream in which one is **cut from the wreckage of a car crash.** In the most frequently occurring version of the dream you lie prone in a twisted seat, bent nearly double and all but immobile, folded like a doll and pinned in the wreckage of a crashed car. The air is filled with the sound of sirens and static whilst all around the rescue services are working, using complex equipment, ripping the twisted metal, cutting with oxyacetylene torches, cutting, tearing and burning. The dream is that of happiness transformed into a prison, a gilded cage at home or at work from which the dreamer must escape. If **someone holds your hand as you lie trapped in the wreckage, comforting you and whispering stories,** you will have an accomplice in your efforts to effect change in your life. If **the car is burning** you will hurt others as you escape.

The dream has a mirror, a reversal of roles in which **you are walking on a road at night and discover the scene of a car crash.** There is smoke in the air, crushed windscreen glass underfoot. With a rising feeling of panic and nausea you slowly realise that **the person lying crumpled and trapped in the concertina'd form of the car is a loved one** (spouse, lover, sibling, offspring). The dream speaks of a conflict soon to be faced – choosing between your own happiness or that of family and friends. If **the loved one's eyes are closed** the dream predicts a long and difficult journey by night is on the cards. If **the loved one is lying beside a stranger in the wreckage of the car** the dream predicts troubles born of secrecy.

37

Car in Front of You Has Dysfunctional Tail-Lights

The dream tells that a friend or colleague that you have relied on for advice and a sense of direction will badly let you down.

Car Seats from which the Temporary Polythene Coverings have Never been Removed

To dream that your car seats are still covered in this flimsy and miserly way is to know that caution will most certainly betray you. Hesitations at work, worries or doubts in your romantic life and the nervous cancellation of leisure plans all follow this dream bringing repercussions of an unexpected magnitude and strength.

A striking variation of this dream is that in which you are offered the chance to purchase a car in which the seats have been fully upholstered in human skin. To purchase this disquieting vehicle is a good omen, boding well for family and close friends. To refuse to purchase it or worse yet, to haggle over the price, is an omen of certain disaster. Before his downfall and execution the doomed dictator Nicolae Ceausescu famously dreamed of a Mercedes upholstered in this unusual way, recording his dream in a letter to his son. 'The car stood on the forecourt of a garage on Titania Prospect and a salesman was showing me the features,' he wrote. 'I remarked upon the upholstery and he described it with great pleasure and conviction as that made from human skin … My dear son, I left the forecourt without buying the car and have been troubled by the thought of it ever since.' Ceausescu lived but three days after his dream.

Car Wash

To dream of a car wash suggests that the dreamer should think again about a devious or unethical course of action he or she has planned.

If the dreamer works in a car wash or runs a business that operates them then the dream has a

38

different significance; predicting holidays, sick-leave or early retirement.

Car with the Headlights Left On

Seen **in daylight** a car with its headlights left on augurs ill for those with children, well for those in commerce and offers mixed fortunes to all who would travel.

Seen at **night time** a car with its headlights left on predicts a whirlwind romance.

If the **headlights are severely drained and fading** the dream predicts disruption, war and illness.

If the **headlights are in a last burst of brilliance** before final extinction the dream predicts sudden inspiration.

Carpet Bombing

A job will be well planned and thoroughly done.

Carpet Burns

Domestic violence, danger at close quarters.

Cartoons

Any serious account of the pains, pleasures and significances of Modern Dreaming must pay tribute to the persistent, yet strangely osmotic, influence exerted from the world of animated cartoons.

In many dreams the events of cartoons **merge directly with those of the subject's life**, whilst in others **the real world becomes suddenly and inexplicably subject to the physics and logic of the animated universe.** In these dreams violence is the rule, physical distortion the convention and destruction at the end of almost every road. Who has not dreamed of **walking off a building and then continuing quite happily into mid-air until chancing to look down?** Or of **bumping one's head on a telegraph pole and then shattering into a thousand pieces like so much ultra-fine china?** Each of these dreams is a warning: to look twice at any situation, to read the small print, to check figures, to look closely into a lover's eyes.

Dreams in which **solid materials and objects bend** (walls, banisters, garden tools, ornaments) and **take on extraordinarily plastic qualities** (bending, warping, extending, stretching) are reminders of the need for compromise and negotiation in one's life, whilst dreams in which **the human body itself is subject to such malleable distortions** (stretching, perforating, compacting, morphing) are warnings not to take on too much at work or at home, or else, in the case of a politician, predictions of mishap, assasination plots or terrorist bombs.

We may not easily forget the unique *visual and auditory* textures of cartoon dreams. The vivid colours of modern animation (violent violets, lime greens, neon reds and migraine yellows) often appear out of context in dreams, adding a lurid spin to scenes that are otherwise apparently realistic and banal in form and content. In such cartoon-coloured dreams the meaning is bound up in the precise make-up and hue of the colours. If the world tends to **blue** the dream is a reminder to pay a visit to an old, neglected friend or of outstanding payments, fines and debts; if the world tends to **red** the dream is a reminder of the need for financial caution and if the world tends to the **green** the dream is a warning of illness or infection in oneself or one's immediate family.

There are also frequent Modern Dreams in which one's **blind and blundering journey through a dark or muted non-space is accompanied by a comical soundtrack of cartoon origin** – whoops, fanfares, explosions, bird-whistles, symphonic crescendos, menacing stutters from cello and violin, twittering birds, peels of laughter, yowls of superhuman pain. Such dreams warn against unwise investment, insincerity in a friend, uncertainty in a lover and lack of substance in a building or bridge. The louder the sounds the more ominous the warning.

See also **Finger in the End of a Shotgun** *and* **Mickey Mouse**

Cash Register	The dream foretells money lost to gambling, ill-considered investments and unwise ventures.
Catchphrases	A dream peppered with catchphrases is an omen of fame.

Common is the dream in which a catchphrase must be **remembered or spoken repeatedly to gain access to some dream building**. If the dreamer **succeeds** in remembering the catchphrase the dream portends harmonious times ahead. If the dreamer **does not succeed** the dream is an omen of strife.

Catwalk Show	A parade of models in unlikely garments down a runway in Paris, New York or Milan indicates that you will have fair, just and healthy children.

If the **models stumble** or the **crowd boos** the meaning of the dream is reversed.

A dream of a catwalk show at which **Sophia Loren, Madonna** or **Ivana Trump** is present foretells of happiness and riches.

Cat with Fireworks Tied to its Tail

The appearance of this shivering, shell-shocked and singed creature in a dream is a powerful, good omen.

If the cat **makes a howling noise** your business will prosper.

If its **eyes dart everywhere** your social calendar will be full.

See also **Animals** *and* **Birds Sitting on Telephone Wires**

Cavity Wall	A friend will keep a secret from you.
CCTV	To dream of watching your life from the distant and near-vertical perspective of CCTV predicts a trial or other investigation.

If the **images are stuttering,** playing one frame in every ten, the dream foretells hold-ups, delays, procrastination.

To see the familiar landscape of **your own bedroom in the strange context of wide-angle**

CCTV means that you will get a visit from a long lost friend.

If there are **many people moving in the bedroom** the friend may not stay very long.

Censored Film

The dream depends for its meaning on the *method* of the censorship.

If **offending scenes or shots have simply been removed,** creating problems with continuity, rhythm or narrative flow, the dream indicates disruption in the domestic life of the dreamer.

If the censorship has been effected by the presence of a **pixelated area or areas on screen which move around to follow the faces or genitals of the actors** then the dream stands for something hidden in the house or garden of the dreamer, which must be found at all costs.

If a film has been censored **to remove all mention or occurrences of death** then the dreamer will face hardships at the workplace or on holiday.

Closely related to these dreams of censorship is that in which programmes scheduled for broadcast on state TV have been **replaced without notice or explanation by a lengthy and tedious classical concert.** In life this action occurs chiefly in situations of revolution or public disorder, but in a dream the bland concert, broadcast not to reveal truth but to obscure it, indicates a conflict in the heart of the dreamer.

See also **X-Rated Movies**

Censored Mail

To dream that someone is censoring your mail suggests that you are frightened to tell the truth.

If **verbs** are censored the dream predicts the onset of blindness.

If **adjectives** are censored the dream means that a loss of control is in the offing.

If **names alone** are censored the dreamer will die.

Cervical Smear

A common Modern Dream which predicts a good holiday.

42

Chainlink Fencing Steadfastness and constancy in love; sturdiness in family and friends.

Changing Clothes in a Telephone Booth

Duplicities in public; a good end achieved by dubious means.

Channel Hopping Indecision, frustration, procrastination.

To dream that **someone else controls the blipper**, channel-hopping in a sequence and a rhythm quite alien to your own, is a dream predicting bad sex.

Cheerleaders A dream of cheerleaders, with short identical skirts and boundless enthusiasm, is a warning not to accept bribes or flattery or to believe the promises of strangers.

Similar dreams are those of **whole teams of eager press and PR people or swarms of dedicated young gofers, interns and assistants.**

If cheerleaders are **wearing glasses** the meaning of the dream is reversed.

Chemotherapy A dream of good health. The more intensive the chemo and the more severe the damage it wreaks in terms of hair loss, blurred vision and headaches, the better one's health will be.

If **people are staring at one's discoloured skin or balding head** the dream warns of an unsettled relationship with the past.

Chewing Gum Dream chewing gum derives its meaning from the places in which it has been stuck.

On **the bottom of a chair** it stands for financial great fortune, whilst **stuck on the bottom of your shoe** it stands for a sporting success. If the gum is **hardened,** the omen is certain. If it **retains a softness or moisture** then the future predicted may be malleable.

If you dream of chewing gum **entwined in your fingers or stretched between your mouth and that of another** there will be a complicated dispute about a will, lease or other legal matter.

A dream of **a girl or a youth using chewing gum**

to blow bubbles is a dream which anticipates an amorous encounter of a worldly kind.

A dream of a pavement or sidewalk polka-dotted with chewing-gum spots is a dream that is highlighting a chance for a revolution – the masses will rise up and claim their long overdue inheritance.

Chicken The dreamer stands in the path of an oncoming vehicle with a friend or lover beside him. The first to dive for safety is a chicken. The dream portends loss.

Chicken Cooked in Tango

Fear of innovation, mistrust of the future.

See also **Bathing in Diet Lilt, Cut Your Finger and Pepsi Comes Out** *and* **Diet Pepsi**

Child Borne Away by an Escalator

The dream that a child loses hold of your hand in a department store and strays onto an escalator, borne away by its slow yet inevitable motion, crying and unable to move, is a common Modern Dream.

If the child has vanished when you chase after it to the next floor the dream foretells of a wound or an infection.

If the child is waiting at the top playing happily with some much-loved toy, then the dream predicts a happy journey.

A similar dream is to lose a small child who has stepped unaccompanied into an elevator and pressed some button or another, ascending or descending to an unknown destination and fate. If you chase through the adjacent stairwells, searching for and finding the child, the dream signifies a mishap involving kitchens, gardens or a valued ornament. If the elevator returns bearing not the child but its clothes the dream portends a revelation and, most probably, a loss.

Chinese Take-Away
> Peace and harmony are predicted. The dreamer will find a winning balance of healthy desires, wealth and energies.

Chocolate Money Eating disorders, gambling addictions, unsettled relations with friends.
> *See also* **Visa Card will not Swipe, Currency Changes** *and* **Money Stolen or Eaten by a Vending Machine**

Chocolate Nooses The dream of this morbid confectionery is a sign of wealth following grief. The grief will be short, the wealth full and long-lasting.

Christmas Eve in Accident & Emergency
> Thronged with punchy drunks bedecked in tinsel, Santa hats and bloody noses, the dream features many important symbols of great significance, whose appearance in diverse combinations make this dream a classic of the Modern genre.
>
> There is the **Man who Still Wants a Fight** (persistence in love), **the Mouthy Girlfriend of the Man who has had his Foot Run Over by a Taxi** (skill in rhetoric, success in politics or sales) and her inconstant companion **the Man who has had his Foot Run Over by a Taxi** (success in the field of athletics), the **Comatose Man**, laid out uncomfortably on the bright green plastic seating (death and serious illness); there is the **Taxi Driver's Daughter** (secret romance) and the **Weeping Orderly** (secret troubles), the **Bank Official who Thinks he might have Just Had a Heart Attack** (failure in love) and the **Black Bloke who is Not Really Speaking to Anyone** (divisions in family, city or state).
>
> If there is **blood on the tiled floor** the meaning of the dream tends generally to the good.
>
> If **the mood is sombre and quiet** the meaning of the dream tends more generally to the bad.
>
> If there are **drunks** in the dream who are **singing a version of 'Hark The Herald Angels**

Sing' with the words changed to something dirty the dream foretells of harmony in unexpected places.

Christmas has Come Too Early

It is summer and the skies are light well into the evenings and yet council workmen are fixing the Christmas decorations and great strings of flashing lights to the buildings and the street-lamps. This common Modern Dream of Christmas coming too early signifies danger, especially in matters concerning finance.

Cider Boys   *See* Winos

Circle of Onlookers

The streets of many Modern Dreams are haunted by groups of onlookers, who have gathered in a circle and are staring intently inward at some event in the heart of their number. The meaning of the dream is determined by the nature of the action at its centre.

If the mob has gathered round a man who is having a heart attack the dream foretells of emotional upsets, tears and confrontations in the weeks ahead.

If the crowd has gathered around an unfortunate soul who is suffering an epileptic fit the dream predicts setbacks and disappointment in the progress of one's career.

To dream that a crowd has gathered round a lost child predicts a visit to a major urban centre (New York, Paris, London); whilst a dream in which a circle of pedestrians has gathered around an old man with a twisted ankle and a pair of split and spilled shopping bags predicts a poor performance in some assessment, task, test or examination.

If there are broken eggs or cracked jars and canned goods rolling on the pavement the meaning of the dream is reversed.

If one finds oneself lying on concrete paving slabs, staring up into the eyes of strangers, in the

46

centre of a voyeuristic circle, the dream signifies a birth.

Circuit Board A circuit board in a dream is a symbol of the city in miniature. If the circuit board is **new, complex and beautiful** the dream predicts law and good order, pride and prosperity for its citizens.

To dream of a circuit board which is **dirty, cracked and chipped** predicts chaos for the city which will suffer crime, refuse or other utility strikes, and an increase in suicides.

Circuit Diagram If the diagram is of **a simple rheostat** the dream is an omen of good fortune arising from a well-prepared plan.

If it shows the **complex interior of a bomb** the dream foretells of change.

A dream of a **vast and incomprehensible** circuit diagram, annotated in pencil marks, with erasures, notes and calculations predicts a future full of plans which will surely fail. The dreamer must learn to improvise, to take things as they come.
See also **Quango**

Circuit Training A dream of running in circles at dawn speaks of thrills and excitements turned into routines.

If one **runs wearing a branded/designer/logoed tracksuit** the routine will lead to success.

To see **one's breath form strange patterns as one jogs around the track** is an omen of danger ahead.

Cling Film To dream of **objects wrapped in cling film** reverses their meaning. In particular the meaning and impact of a dream of **bad omens** (such as **binoculars, car bombs, fish fingers** or **bum-bags**) can be lessened or neutered in this way.

To dream of **one's friends wrapped in cling film** warns of a quarrel over money or a dispute about intimate secrets; the more layers of cling film the more serious the quarrel.

Clinging to the Runners of the Chopper as it takes off from the Embassy Roof　If the dreamer manages to cling on to the chopper or is pulled aboard by colleagues the dream predicts joyous events. If the dreamer looks down and sees the burning streets of Saigon alive with people running and fighting the dream is at its strongest. If the city is blurred or indistinct the joy predicted will be that much the less.

　　　　　If the dreamer loses his or her handhold on the chopper runners, or is shot down by enemy troops, plunging to the ground far below, the dream predicts a practical joke that will go wrong.

Clock Radio　Children in trouble, the start and end of stories, precision at work.

Clothes Drying on a Radiator

Unkindness in relatives, richness in worldly goods, wisdom from travel.

Coal-Effect Electric Bar Fire

The plastic coals and surrounding 'fire' – textured black forms in a lurid sea of dubious orange – change colour as a tiny convection fan hidden below rotates slowly, casting shadows with a half-hearted flickering effect. The dream is of friendship made, strengthened or regained.

Cobain, Kurt　Cobain is a symbol of both music and emptiness. A dream of him predicts a night at a rock venue or, if you are planning a journey, the danger of running out of food or other sustenance.

Coffee Table Books

Your ambition will be thwarted, your faith tested and your shortcomings exposed.

Coins Down the Back of the Sofa

You will not be rich.

Coins in the Urinal

To dream of coins discarded in the rank sediment of a public urinal is to dream that one's hopes and wishes for the future will certainly be dashed.

If the coins are **foreign** the disappointment will be particularly great.

Coins Rejected by a Pay & Display Machine

Minor accidents will befall you which may surprise by leading to permanent change.

See also **Money Stolen or Eaten by a Vending Machine, Visa Card will not Swipe, Currency Changes** *and* **Chocolate Money.**

Cold Calling   You will prosper or suffer at the whim of strangers.

Collateral Damage   You will suffer at the whim of strangers.

Collecting Dog Shit in a Polythene Bag

A dream of humiliation. The dreamer leads or follows some beast around the park, waiting for it to defecate. The meaning of the dream lies mostly in the *waiting*.

A **long wait** means great suffering; a **wait endured under the watchful eyes of other park users** means confrontation at home. To dream of **standing with a fellow dog-owner as you wait for your respective pets to produce a turd** predicts an unstable or ill-fated marriage.

If the dog shit **feels warm as you grip it lightly through the polythene bag** which you have brought along for this purpose the dream warns of urgent matters left long unattended. If the shit **feels cold or hard,** the dream predicts unhappiness in travels.

A dream of **collecting dog shit from the floor in some indoor location** – hotel foyer, office block, supermarket or car showroom – the dream denotes secrets combined with great happiness.

Composing Muzak

Peace, reconciliation by day. Forgetting and silence by night.

Compressed Air   Trouble caused by friends with big mouths.

Computer Code   *See* **Source Code**

Computer Nerds   *See* **Nerds**

Computer Simulation

Desire born from misunderstanding.

Conference Call   Predicts that you will be plagued by extraordinary cares. Any dream of a phone call involving more than two people is a premonition of unavoidable pain.

See also **Talking to your Parents on the Speakerphone**

Confused by the Prices at a Motorway Services

You will be rich.

Contact Lenses   If the lenses are **scratched** you see the present less clearly but you should trust your feelings and hunches about the future.

If the dream involves a **lost** contact lens you should question your judgement in matters of the heart and of finance.

A dream of **tinted** contact lenses is a dream of sincerity.

Control-Alt-Delete

Your lover will betray you.

Controversial Extension, New Wing or Amendment to a Major Public Building   You will be besieged by requests from family, demands from strangers and questions from neighbours.

To dream that **your own home is graced with an extension best described as a provocative architectural intervention and described by many as an eyesore and a carbuncle** predicts unsettled days in the spheres of courtship and career.

Conversation about Taxes

The meaning of the dream arises from the *context* in which the conversation happens.

If the conversation takes place **during sexual intercourse** it is an omen of particular good luck.

If the conversation is **over the telephone** you will get bad news from a relative.

50

A dream of a conversation about taxes **which takes place as one sits by a fire on an urban wasteground** foretells of success in the bedroom.

Convex Security Mirror

To see your **face** reflected in a convex security mirror signifies hardship and an uncertain future.

Cooling Towers A dream of cooling towers tells the dreamer to keep his or her temper carefully controlled in the days ahead.

If the cooling towers are **half obscured by fog** the dream stands for futures in the balance: decisions and ambitions that may not be achieved.

Co-Presenter is Behaving Strangely

A dream which predicts difficulties in a complex financial arrangement.

If your co-presenter is **corpsing continually** the difficulties will be largely contractual.

If he or she **looks nervous, edgy and possibly desperate to go to the toilet** the financial difficulties will concern a mortgage or land purchase.

If he or she is **talking ten-to-the-dozen and skipping way off the end of the autocue** financial difficulties will be exacerbated by personal indiscretions.

Corpse Rolled Up in an Old Carpet That's Tied Up with String

Your romance, which looked so promising, will eventually fail.

Couch Potato To dream that you are a great big lardarse couch potato and you get out of breath when you have to go upstairs or even go and answer the door is a dream predicting the opposite – fitness, health and sporting success.

Counterfeit Jeans A dream of counterfeit jeans signifies an argument with neighbours, especially if the **stitching is defective or weak**.

If the jeans are being **stored or sold from the**

back of a van the dream predicts hardship with commerce and taxation.

Courtesy Telephone

A dream that one is called to a courtesy telephone foretells of loss of memory, the loss of a fortune or gains by gambling or the stock exchange.

Cover Version(s)   The dream depends for its meaning on the songs covered.

If they are **punk songs** the dream means an early end to well-loved projects; if they are **country tunes** the dream predicts a situation in which you will have to act from principle. If the cover versions are **standards** the dream predicts a situation that is new to you and at the same time very well known.

See also **Impressed by a Tribute Band or Solo Impersonator**

Cowboy Builders   Contentment will come to those who dream of a firm of cowboy builders.

If the men are **bodging a roof** your contentment will stem from wise investments.

If the men are **brewing tea in the back of their transit van, exchanging dirty jokes and cadging fags off each other** your contentment will be shortlived.

Crane Shot   The dream foretells the need to gain a better perspective.

If the crane **rises rapidly,** affording a bird's-eye view of some internal or external location, you will gain such perspective with ease.

If the crane shot **has to be repeated due to technical difficulties or a problem with the choreography of the extras,** you will struggle to keep the perspective you so desire.

To see **your own self** in a crane shot – looking down at your prone figure lying on a bed or on some grassy bank – is a premonition of early death.

Craze of Whistling

A lone man starts the craze, making bird song from his window on the thirtieth floor of some tall apartment building in the projects. Within days there are hundreds of whistlers, filling the night sky with song, and children love it but it drives the adults crazy. Each night the noise of it gets louder as more people join the craze and lean from their windows in the dark to whistle. The nights become magical, beautiful with this sound, noisier than daytime and real birds fly disoriented, confused by the sound. In the end the mayor goes on TV and cries, weeping and weeping, 'Stop it, stop it, stop it, stop the whistling' and 'Is this birdland? Is this birdland?' and then you awake. The dream is one of transformation. A person or a place you are bored with will soon be reinvented in your eyes.

Crazy Golf

A dream of strange challenges, chiefly in the context of work. The dreamer will need to think hard, act fast and keep cool to succeed as new rules and new situations must be met and conquered far from his or her normal routine.

If the course for the crazy golf is **painted in bright colours** the dream is also a warning of serious danger.

To dream of being **beaten by a child at crazy golf** portends demotion or dismissal.

A dream in which the dreamer **gambles insistently**, upping the stakes and wagering first money, then possessions, house, family members and ultimately his or her soul on the outcome of a game of crazy golf, is a disquieting dream of a sense of proportion which has been lost. The dreamer needs to take time, take heed and re-evaluate.

Crazy Paving

If the lines in the crazy paving **seem to form cryptic letters or words** the dream is one of secrecy established between friends or broken between lovers.

To dream that **the lines formed by crazy paving**

create a complex maze is to predict a direction which, once found, will only be lost again.

Credits Sequence/End Titles

A dream in the form of a **credits sequence** means that a new chapter in one's life is about to begin.

By contrast a dream in the form of an **end titles sequence** predicts a premature ending for love or work.

The dream of the **final scrolling credits** in a movie, with **names in white letters scrolling evenly and with inevitable precision up and off the pitch-black screen** is a reminder of missed opportunities. The more names appear in the credits the more the dreamer has to regret.

See also **Jump Cuts**

Crocodile Clips

The course of events will be altered by an animal or animals in unexpected places.

Crop Circles

Supposedly mysterious spiral and circle formations appearing spontaneously overnight in fields of growing wheat or corn have only minor significance in a dream, predicting small success for farmers and those in agricultural administration or politics.

Crowd of Office Workers Smoking Outside an Office Building

The dream portends a disaster. The more people there are smoking the worse the disaster will be. If the workers are smoking **on the fire escape** there will be a death. If they are **shivering** the disaster will bring unexpected benefits for the dreamer alone.

Cruise Missiles

A sexual dream. You will embark on a long-distance relationship.

If the missiles are **in their silos** you will have great pleasure.

Cult

To dream of joining a cult **oneself** signifies danger from electricity, financial mismanagement and sporting injury.

54

A dream in which one's **son or daughter** joins a cult foretells a difficult family occasion – a Christmas beset by strife, a wedding marred by feuding, or a christening that ends in a punch-up.

There are many Modern Dreams in which the dreamer joins a cult that **insists on sexual liberation, the sharing of personal possessions or a round the clock rota of arduous chores.** To **surrender** to such diverse conditions is a promise of happiness achieved through hard work and dedication.

Culture Shock   A visit from strangers.

Cure for Cancer   To dream that **you have invented a cure for cancer** is an insignificant dream which predicts an amicable end to a long running if trivial argument.

Currency Changes   The dreamer is typically confused by some seemingly pointless change in the currency. This may involve **decimalization** or it may involve **conversion to the Euro.** Alternatively, the changes dreamt of may simply arise from the **introduction of new coins or banknotes.**

In each instance the meaning of the dream is the same: if the dreamer is a woman she will have unexpected trouble with men. If the dreamer is a man he will have unexpected trouble with children.

To dream of currency **that one cannot recognise, with lurid designs, preposterous denominations and unknown portraits on the back and front of the notes** predicts a marriage.

See also **Everyday Item has been Needlessly Re-designed or Re-packaged**

Custard Pie Fight   Slapstick, with its strange ambivalent play between cruelty, chaos and comedy, is a deep force in Modern Dreams, and the classic custard pie fight is a powerful and frequent occurrence. The meaning of the dream is best understood if one thinks of the custard pies as memories. The more pies hit the dreamer the more he or she will have to deal with

55

the residues and consequences of actions in the past.

If the pies **strike the dreamer in the face** the memories will be of conversations or kisses; if they **strike in the chest** they will be of love or illness, if they strike in the **region below the waist** they will be of sex or of children.

Other common **slapstick dreams** include **big shoes** (trouble with the law), **dropping a piano down three flights of stairs** (a need for greater harmony and peace, a need for holidays), **running through a pane of glass** (a warning of dangers ahead), **the ladder gag** (prediction of a rise to great fortune) and **the bow tie that spins** (changes in the dreamer's romantic inclinations) or **the bow tie that squirts water** (grief of a horrible, continuous and melancholy kind).

See also **Bucket of Water on Top of a Door**

Cut Your Finger and Pepsi Comes Out
Misadventures, mischief, buffoonery.

See also **Diet Pepsi, Chicken Cooked in Tango** *and* **Diet Lilt**

D

Dad Asleep in Front of the TV
You will be cared for, loved and cherished without
pause, end or condition.

Dadaists   A dream of disquiet. Upheaval, quick change, the
present shrouded in a fog of delirium.

Daleks   To dream of the Daleks, terrifying anti-heroes of
the popular BBC television series *Dr Who*, signifies
trouble with an ageing relative.
See also **Invented Creatures**

Dallas Book Depository
A dream of the Dallas Book Depository signals an
end to cherished plans. If the window from which
shots were supposedly fired is circled informatively
in red the end will be sudden and unexpected.

Dance Marathon   The room is large and dark, with a vaulted ceiling
and no windows, so there is no way of telling
whether it is night or day outside. The dreamer and
other dancers wear numbers, whilst the dancing
itself, a weary, exhausted shuffle, seems to have
been going on for many many days. The dream
stands for orthodoxy and expresses the need to
rebel. For the most part the music is upbeat whilst
the dancing is slow. If there are variations the
meaning of the dream changes.
   Frenetic dancing stands for inconstancy.
   If the tune is **'Closer My Lord To Thee'** the
dream signifies success in secret but heartfelt
endeavours. If the tune is **'Love Boat'** the dream
signifies travel plans that will have to be
abandoned. As in the common dream of **riding in
the Tour de France** the dancer (or rider) who wears

57

the number 66 will have good fortune, while the riders (or dancers) wearing 3, 5, 7 or 9 will have bad fortune.

To dream that a dancer collapses, a cacophony of crumpled legs and arms, warns of the need for caution when approaching strangers, tests, or new opportunities.

Dangerous Fairground Ride

The meaning of the dream lies in the identity of your companion or companions.

To face some rickety, speeding and unstable ride with your parents at your side betokens a shady transaction at work or at school.

To take the ride with a lover predicts an end to the easy part of your relationship and the onset of problems.

To take a dangerous fairground ride, lurching over unstable timbers to the sound of tape-recorded screams, in the company of strangers predicts a disreputable business transaction or a legal victory achieved through bribery.

Darkness

The Modern world has given birth to many new species of darkness; some partial, others complete, each of which has its own unique meaning and interpretation.

To dream of the kind of darkness inside an elevator in which the lights have failed is to dream of a new beginning in work or in love.

A dream of the darkness inside a deep freeze refrigerator foretells of troubles in parks, gardens or on beaches.

A dream of the darkness in a car parked up beside a minor road, waiting in a lay-by in total silence, is a dream that augurs well for travel or murder.

The shifting and uneasy darkness in the trunk of a car, or the soft darkness between projections in a cinema both augur well for marriage plans and secret investigations.

58

In some dreams the meaning is not so much in the location as in the combination of it and other things glimpsed – to see **flashes in the darkness of an underground carpark** predicts car crime, drug deals or success in singing love songs. To see **stars or shimmering pinpricks of light in the heavy darkness of a flotation tank** is a dream signifying that hope should not be abandoned.

Perhaps best known of all Modern Dreams of darkness is that of darkness **in a department store at night**. This dream, with its particular soundscape of footsteps on the carpet, the whispering of fountains and the soft purr of escalators working endlessly unseen in the distance foretells that the dreamer will find religious faith.

Finally we must turn to the dream of the darkness **experienced by game show contestants as they wait blindfolded in a soundproof booth**. The dream predicts deceit.

| Date Rape | A dream of its opposite – true love, deep and long lasting. |

A dream of its opposite – true love, deep and long lasting.

If the rape is **multiple** the union will be blessed by many children.

See also **Rape Alarm**

Dating Agency

To dream that you are searching through the files of a dating agency, staring at the carefully chosen photographs and reading statements about the hobbies of those pictured, is a dream which foretells of uncertainty, not in love but in business.

If the subjects offered are **attractive** you must be decisive, if they are **plain** you may contemplate a merger or management buy-out.

To dream of potential partners who are **ugly** or **deformed** predicts bankruptcy and a speedy end to the business in question.

Dawn Raid

To dream the arrival of police or immigration officers with sledge hammers at dawn foretells a birth in the family.

If the raiders are **customs officers** the birth may be of twins.

Day-Glow Colours

A generally fortunate dream, whether indoors or out, especially if the colours are **painted on one's skin.**

Daylight Dreams   Daylight Dreams, in which the events of night-time are transposed to daylight, are as common in the Modern repertoire as their meaning is hotly debated. To some the unexpected clarity of the night's events, revealed in the brilliance of sunshine suggests a revelation or breakthrough of a scientific kind whilst for others the shifting of night to day suggests an instability or potential for reversal in the fortunes of the dreamer. The true meaning of a Daylight Dream lies in its humidity, since often the unexpected daylight brings a warmth and rise in moisture levels. If **the heat and moisture is agreeable** the dream bodes well; if it is **unpleasant,** causing sweats and discomfort, the dream bodes ill. A Daylight Dream in which **torches, floodlights and car headlamps are all switched on, despite the glaring sunshine,** predicts the arrival of a stranger bearing curious news.

See also **Buying a VCR from the Boot of a Car**

Dayton Accord   To dream of the Dayton Accord (also called the Dayton Agreement) denotes compromise and impotency.

Death Has Been Unwittingly Captured On Amateur Video

You will have many children. If you have children already they will prosper. The more bloody and violent the death in the dream the more children you will have, or the more success your existing children will have.

See also **Home Movie Has Unwittingly Captured a Historical Event**

Debt Collectors   Someone will offer you flattery.

Declaring Love by Loud Hailer
You will be ridiculed.

Decorative Plasterwork Borders of Flowers, Rabbits and Birds high up near the Ceiling have been Buried, Lost and Blurred by the accretion of years and years of Thickly and Carelessly Applied Thick White Emulsion
The dream is one of forgetting, of lost clarity or lost direction.

If the eyes of the plasterwork rabbits are blocked with the layers of paint you will suffer a crisis in your career, a plunge from favour or an injury.

If the flowers seem to drip beads of dried emulsion paint like dew drops or tears you will weep deep in the night and early in the morning.

Defending Yourself with a Dustbin Lid
Someone will offer you very bad advice.

Deregulation of Public Utilities
To a mother or a father this dream foretells the breakdown and slow transformation of domestic affairs, especially in relation to meal-times. The family will eat alone increasingly, or in front of the television. Meals that were once social occasions will become solitary meetings with the cardboard crockery of the takeaway pizza box.

If the dream involves the deregulation of the water supply the washing up in your house will be neglected for weeks.

Deserted Airport Like the dream of a deserted railway terminal this dream indicates that your travel plans may be thwarted by plague or industrial action amongst ground control staff or maintenance workers.

A breeze blowing in the depopulated concourses indicates a possible early end to the dispute.

Diana, Princess of Wales
Diana, Princess of Wales died young and tragically in a motor crash in a Paris underpass, ensuring her a place in the hearts of the population and in the make-up of our Modern psyches forever. To dream of Diana is to anticipate your own death.

61

Diet Pepsi	A dream of Diet Pepsi foretells that your life will soon be both sweeter and better for you. *See also* **Chicken Cooked in Tango, Bathing in Diet Lilt** *and* **Cut Your Finger and Pepsi comes out**
Digital Clock	You are wasting time and energy on a foolish and unproductive project.
Dirty Faxes	A dream of **sending dirty faxes** – anonymous, suggestive, crude and offensive – is a sign of trouble ahead, illnesses of ageing relatives, or surprises from friends. To dream of **receiving a dirty fax** augurs well for the dreamer and all connected to her or him.
Dirty Weekend	The dream of a dirty weekend is a warning against greed. If the dirty weekend takes place in an **English bed and breakfast at the seaside** you are being especially greedy.
Disco Revival	The dream augurs ill for those in commerce but well for those in industry.
Discothèque	The flashing lights, up-tempo music, fluorescent bathrooms, darkened booths and raised dance floors of discothèques provide the setting for many Modern Dreams. If the discothèque is **crowded** you will be popular and happy. If its stages, bars and corridors are **empty** you will face old age alone. Most ominous is the dream in which the **other dancers clear the floor for you, surrounding you as you dance, making space and gathering around, clapping, whooping and whistling**. To **stop** dancing in this situation foretells of a crisis in your business affairs but to **continue** foretells of illness, agony and despair. *See also* **Bouncers, Breakdancing, Foam Party**

Disguised Celebrity

To dream of a celebrity in disguise portends a sudden transformation in the form of a makeover or clothes shopping trip.

If the celebrity **speaks directly to the dreamer** the dream predicts the sharing and breaking of a secret, or signifies a hidden problem in the dreamer's life or that of a close friend.

In many such dreams the celebrity will **wear thick and large dark glasses, a headscarf or baseball cap and a voluminous floor-length coat.** The more all-engrossing the disguise the more the dream tends to the dangerous, the unspeakable and the hidden.

If the celebrity **implores the dreamer not to reveal their identity** the dream signals hard times on the horizon, money troubles or a crisis of confidence.

A dream in which a celebrity **whisks away from a hotel pushed hurriedly in a large coat to the back seat of a car** is a dream of fear, a problem which needs to be solved or a person in the dreamer's life who must be avoided.

Dishwasher

You will receive a letter.

Dissolving Stitches

A dream in which one is injured and then the wounds are stitched with dissolving stitches foretells of the disappearance of a friend, a workmate or a neighbour.

If the stitches are **small in number** the disappearance may be that of a child.

To dream that **one's mouth is sealed** with dissolving stitches is a warning to keep secrets and to trust no one.

Disposable Camera

The dream is telling you to take a good look at yourself in the mirror one day and have a serious think about where you are heading.

Disposable Nappies

Struggles in the bedroom, successes in the boardroom.

Disposable Razors

Hatred, hostility, random violence.

Divergent Thinking Test

The dream foretells of a period of mental aberration and fixity.

Divorce
The dream warns of misleading happiness.

If the divorce is a **quickie-divorce** it augurs well for a woman and badly for a man.

DJ
A dream of a DJ predicts an encounter with a stranger or strangers.

If the DJ is **scratching** the encounter will be pleasant; if he is **talking over the music** and making wise-cracks about the dancing or about people who are going to the toilet and how long they are spending in there the encounter will be tense and difficult.

D.N.A.
The double helix, the basis for all life, represents an extraordinary event in the construction of the contemporary psychic landscape, unique in that its spiral of entwining strands is thus far the only object to have been *first sighted* in a dream – that of Francis Crick, its co-discoverer, who glimpsed the structure of his quarry in the form of intertwining snakes. With an origin of this kind it should come as no surprise that DNA remains a powerful and entrenched symbol in the world of Modern Dreams. A dream of DNA is a dream of the structure of the dreamer's life – not short-order predictions or the sign of a lucky month, week or year. DNA reveals instead the deep trend, the long-term prognosis.

If the strands are coloured **red** and **green** the prognosis is upward and good.

If they are **blue** and **yellow** the prognosis is downwards and bad.

A dream of **taking a DNA test** foretells of a terrible trial or ordeal in the dreamer's life.

Docking a Space Station

A sexual dream.

If the docking is **easy** the sex will be good.

If the docking is **hard** and **the astronauts have to come out of the spaceship and guide the docking mechanism home manually** then the sex will be arduous or useless and there will be a lot of silence and a general lack of eye contact at breakfast the next morning.

Docusoap

The pace of your life will slow to that of an unbearable grind. If the docusoap **has a pregnancy** in it you will suffer an unexpected blow to your confidence.

See also **Rockumentary**

Dog Biscuits

To dream of eating dog biscuits is an auspicious omen of good fortune and success.

If the dog biscuits are formed in a **classic 'cartoon' bone-shape** your success will be sudden; if they are **malformed lumps or pellets in a dish** your success will be hard-won.

Dogs Locked in the Back of a Car

To dream of two dogs trapped in the baking sunlit oven of a parked and locked car is a premonition of conflict.

If the dogs are **active, hysterical and barking** the conflict will be short.

If they are **sleepy and indolent** the conflict will be long and drawn-out, whilst if the dogs are **so ill they are nearing death** the dream portends a conflict ending in fortune and happiness.

A further level of meaning in the dream is both revealed and determined by the make of the car in which the unfortunate animals are incarcerated. A **Mercedes** indicates that the conflict will be a business one. A **Lada**, **Volvo** or **Fiat** indicates that the conflict will be personal.

65

Dole Fraud   Fear, secrecy, shame.

Donkey Kong   Your life is ruled by trivia and for once this will have humorous consequences.

Doors to the Carriage of an Underground Train will not Open
For a man impotence, for a woman the termination of a pregnancy.

Double Glazing   Those installing double glazing in a dream can expect the healing of a personal rift which has distressed or troubled them for some time.

If **a stranger** is installing the double glazing the dream is a warning against idleness.

To be **plagued by a persistent salesman of double glazing** is a warning against giving in to feelings of rage.

Double-Shot Lo-Fat No-Foam Latte
You will visit a far away place and be bitterly disappointed.

Doused in Petrol in a Public Place
A dream of fame.

Dow Jones   If the Market is **up** the dream is a bad omen.

If the Market is **down** the dream predicts good fortune.

See also **Nikkei, Hang Seng** *and* **F.T.S.E.**

Drag Racing   Adventure, loneliness.

Drawing of a Big Battle between two Great Warring Armies, the Paths of Bullets and Bombs represented by Dotted Lines.
These vast drawings, detailed and obsessive, are common in the Modern Dreams of children. The meaning lies in the kind of pen or drawing implement used.

If executed in **biro** the dream predicts the loss of a valuable item, if in **pencil** the arrival of unexpected news from overseas, if in **crayons** the substitution of one love for another, if in **felt pens** a permanent and irreversible change.

Drinking Your Age in Pints

The dream is rare but has great significance.

If the dreamer **succeeds** in drinking his or her age in pints there will be years of good luck, the number of years being equal to the number of pints consumed. If the dreamer is **unsuccessful** in this heroic task there will be years of bad luck, the number of years being equal to the number of pints which have not been drunk. If the dreamer is very old and therefore unlikely to enjoy a further ninety-eight years of good luck it is possible that luck accrued in this dream will be passed on to a spouse, younger sibling or offspring.

If the **pub falls silent** as the dreamer is drinking the meaning of the dream is reversed.

Drive-by Shooting The dream is of good luck; the more bloody the death the better the fortune predicted.

Drive-in Fast Food

A warning dream. You will be praised for something you have not done. To accept the praise will cause trouble and the loss of a friendship.

Drive-in Movie A dream of a drive-in movie provides indications concerning the prospects of future plans.

If **the weather at the drive-in is good and the sky is clear** the dream predicts success in a new venture. If **the weather is inclement** the dream augurs ill for new things but strength to existing projects, relationships and initiatives.

To dream that **one is making out in the flickering half-light of a drive-in movie theatre as the sound of the movie washes over one** predicts an uncertain future, a confusion about truth and illusion or a crisis of spirit and faith.

Driver is Sleeping Common is the Modern Dream that the driver of the car in which the dreamer is travelling is asleep. With a nodding head and heavy, heavy eyes the car drifts from lane to lane, oblivious to the rush of traffic, blurring tail lights and the ricochet of car horns.

If the sleeping driver is **a friend or relation** the dream signifies a continued situation of trust and security.

If the driver is **a stranger** it signifies a penchant for risk in the dreamer, a penchant that must be checked.

A dream in which the driver sleeps for the entire duration of a long, long journey, nodding, muttering and slobbering and yet, somehow, inexplicably, the journey is completed safely with no accidents, no scrapes, no sense of danger beyond a basic unease, is a common dream which foretells that luck will play a major role in the next months of the dreamer's life.

To dream that the driver of a car in which one is travelling is **dead**, turning the wheel with cold hands and a motionless heart, forewarns of a serious accident.

Drowned Giant   To dream of a drowned giant washed up and stranded on a beach is to foresee that one will have a child.

If the giant **soon becomes surrounded by ice cream vendors, burger vans and hot dog stalls, postcard sellers and souvenir stalls** the dream predicts a wealth of children and friends.

Drowning in a Vat of the Luminous Gunk which is Commonly Poured onto Children in Competitive TV Shows

To dream that you are drowning in gunk in this way is to lament the loss of carefree childhood days.

A dream in which **your offspring** meet this most absurd, tragic and fully public death is a reminder to love them as much as possible while you still have the chance.

Drum Machine   Arrhythmia, spillages, chaos.

Drunk in Legoland

Means your business may fall into a precarious state.

Drunk Man Weeping into a Vocoder, His Tears Coming Out Just Like Words The dream is an inauspicious omen. You will be seduced by flattery in speech, deed or written form.

Drunk to Forget Happy memories will leave a bitter taste.

Drunk to Try and Stop the Pain

Contentment, the silence that comes from satisfaction.

Dual Key System To dream that one **launches a bomb** using the infamous dual key system denotes the affections of a stranger.

If the dream involves **gaining entry to a top security/high security area** using the dual-key system you will cross a boundary of politeness or etiquette without meaning to.

E

Ear Defenders   Solitude by choice, deception by rumour, silence or shadows.

Eating Catseyes   Commonly the dreamer sees him or herself naked, in some primal/feral state, prising catseyes from their rubberised housings in the centre of the road, fingers and fingernails torn and bleeding. The catseyes, once found, are devoured in frenzied ravenous motion, the glass beads slipping down like ice-cold confectionery. The dream signifies thirst for knowledge, a love of animals or a mistrust of technology.

Eating a Microwave, Component by Component

A dream of adapting. The dreamer will meet some new situation or challenge by changing, or by finding new resources and gaining unexpected skills.

If the component parts of the microwave are eaten **whole** the dreamer will be bullish, headstrong, uncompromising.

If the parts are **sawn up, filed down** or **compacted** the dreamer will succeed through dogged persistence.

The dream has a close parallel in those of drinking or eating contests staged for charity or for advertising purposes. A dream of a **contest in which competing teams must eat chocolate guns, butter or money** predicts a future in politics. A dream of a **contest for eating marzipan hearts, houses or traffic lights** foretells success in love, marriage and homemaking for the victor, loss and heartache for the vanquished.

71

Eating at Planet Hollywood
You will be rich and famous.

Eating Pet Food If the pet food is eaten **straight from the can** the
dream signifies determination and the triumph of
sheer will over difficult circumstances.

If the pet food is eaten **cooked (in an omelette,
pie or pastie)** it signifies the importance of planning
and preparation as the dreamer faces trials and
adversities.

To dream that the dreamer eats pet food **without
knowing at the time** warns of a subterfuge at home
or in the office.

Ebay Your actions at work will be studied by a friend.

Ebola You will be happy.

**E.C.G. goes Flatline and Sends Out a Screeching Alarm; the Line
Breaks Up and Turns into a Flock of Lime-Green Birds which then
Proceed to Swoop, Dive and Fly Away**
Immigration, the loss of loved ones, sudden flight
from mortal danger.

Economic Migrants
Forgotten friends, incomplete stories, food shared
with a brother or sister.

Economies of Scale
You will get fat.

Ecstasy Tablet with your Face on it
A warning against giving in to daydreams.

Edible Underwear You will be oppressed by doubts and uncertainties.
If the edible underwear is **soiled** the touchstones
of your life will not make sense anymore, questions
will plague your every waking hour and the solidity
of your friendships and achievements will seem
flimsy and false.

To dream of edible underwear **in a variety of
flavours** foretells a difficult decision with a surfeit
of choices.

72

Eight-Thousand-Piece Jigsaw of the Battle of the Somme in which Each Piece is a Bodypart covered in Mud or Blood, the Dead and the Living almost Indistinguishable as they lie in the Dawn Trenches, Grey Light strafing through Tangles of Barbed Wire

Bad luck combined with hard work. To dream of such a jigsaw foretells of an arduous week ahead for those involved in finances or the law.

To dream that one is **stuck on some particularly difficult corner where a mangled body in filthy khakis lies facedown in a pool of green brackish water** augurs ill for those involved in sports, fitness and psychiatry.

Einstein, Albert The greatest scientific genius of the twentieth century stands for pranks and mischief in a dream.

Election Night Party

A bad dream foretelling financial reverses and ill fortune in the stock market. For lovers it foretells the cessation of all affection.

Electric Chair To dream of death by electric chair predicts strength, good health and prosperity.

If the dream involves **pulling the lever and sending a villain to his death** it predicts fatherhood, or, in the case of a woman, parenting by adoption.

To dream that **one is the doctor called in to verify the time of death** augurs well for those in business, especially the railways.

Electric Fence Invasion of privacy, unexpected intimacies, boundaries of home or family breached.

A dream of **urinating on an electric fence** predicts downfall by sexual indiscretion.

Electric Guitar Insolvency, false dealing, corruption in business.

Electric Power The force of electricity runs deep yet invisible beneath the streets and behind the walls of the Modern world, making it a powerful symbol in the lexicon of slumber.

A dream in which electricity **flows from one**

person to another is a prediction of some important transaction between the two.

If the electricity flows from hand to hand the transaction will be one of business.

If it flows from eye to eye it will be a transaction of love.

If the dream concerns the progress of electricity as it flows from room to room, house to house and street to street, the current visible as a network of pulsing glowing lines, it predicts upheaval in politics, surprise in romance and persuasion in business.

Electronic Hangman

An augury of death.

Electronic Tag

To dream that one's freedom is curtailed by an electronic tag, confining one to home or the immediate neighbourhood is a dream of jealous love. The tighter the curfew restrictions the more jealous the lover will be.

If the tag bracelet creates a rash the love will be short-lived.

Elevator Repair Service

There will be mix-ups, errors and confusions caused by your name or that of a colleague or friend.

Elevator that Stinks of Piss

See Lift that Stinks of Piss *and* Stuck in a Lift Alone

Employed to Help Fill a Quota of Blacks and Asians

A dream of deception and false promises.

If one's colleagues suspect the truth the dream foresees failure in the sexual arena.

If one finds graffiti in the washroom disclosing the context of one's employment the dream predicts a conflict with a sibling or an offspring.

Enola Gay

Change planned in daylight, fermented in darkness.

Entangled in a Complex Copyright Dispute
Bad relations with parents, strife with siblings, dispute with offspring. The dreamer will be dogged by feelings of unbearable closeness.

Error Message 404 not found
The dream speaks of something forgotten which must be remembered at all costs, a name, a phone number, incident, song lyric or sentence.

If 404 Not Found, the common error message from the World Wide Web, **appears repeatedly** the dream has its meaning reversed – that which has been forgotten must remain so at any cost, for evermore.

Error Occurring Whilst Trying to Read the Temporary File
The dream augurs well for those in the giddy first stages of love.

Error of Type 2 The dream warns against spreading your energies too thinly. The combination of work, family and social life you have recently concocted will not work in this way forever. The problem predicted increases in seriousness each time the error message is repeated in a dream.

Eternity by Calvin Klein
The relationship you are in will be quite a long one.
See also **Obsession by Calvin Klein**

Eurodisney A dream of travel. If Eurodisney is **burning** in a dream your travel may be hasty or uncomfortable.

Eurostar from Antwerp to Sheffield
The dream predicts a joke, long and badly told.

Eurovision Song Contest
Bad luck in work and finances.

A dream of **winning the contest** signifies a dispute with neighbours or an argument with friends.

If you are **wearing a costume that exposes your**

midriff the dream predicts a conflict of violent, even military proportions.

Everyday Item has been Needlessly Re-Designed or Re-Packaged
The constant wave of invention, product launches and re-designs from triangular tea-bags through newly-shaped dispensers for bleach to 'advanced' or 'augmented' formulas for toothpaste, baby foods and drinks cause a constant unsettling in the Modern psychic economy. Such re-designed, re-formulated or re-packaged items appear often in dreams, symbols of the strange within the familiar and the inevitability of change.

To dream that one is **searching a supermarket for some everyday purchase, unable to navigate or locate one's prize amongst shelves packed with lurid and unfamiliar re-launched products** is to foresee a change of address.

To dream that **a favourite product has been badly re-designed** predicts a common cold.
See also **Currency Changes**

Everyone in Pizza Hut does a Mexican Wave
This is a dream of great good fortune. To the aspiring pop star it means a record contract, to the whore it means a lot of quick and easy customers, to the tabloid journalist it means a scoop on a hideous tragedy and to the young girl it means a handsome suitor – in brief the dream promises everyone their heart's desire.

If the customers doing the Mexican wave are **wearing Star Wars merchandise** then the whole meaning of the dream is reversed.

Exaggerated Redundancy Package
You will become obese.

Excercycle
You will lose money by needless travels.
See also **Legs Tangled in a Multi-Gym**

Exes Going Past on a Motorised Conveyor Belt
A dream predicting new romance.

Exchange Rates   Transfer of emotions, neglect of duties, loss of inhibitions.

Ex-King Constantine of Greece

You will lose the respect of a family member.

Ex-Lover Calls about the Results of an A.I.D.S. test

Predicts sporting failure, a bout of formal appointments, a change of address or a mass of paperwork to deal with.

Extra in a Big Budget Movie

Unexpected boredom in the midst of an exciting adventure or period of change.

Eyes Blinded by a Hail of Paparazzi Flashes

The dream predicts inspiration, problems solved in sudden breakthroughs after months or years of struggle.

If the paparazzi are **repeatedly calling your name** the dream augurs a crisis or an issue which will need urgent decisions and attention.

Eyes Keep Going to the Top Shelf of Porn Magazines

A dream of reliance on others.

If the **eyes of the models on the magazine covers seem to follow you** the dream predicts a future which must be negotiated with a partner, constantly and carefully.

If the **models have had pubic hair, armpit hair and nipples removed using PhotoShop ©** the dream warns of blandness, a weak will and the problems caused by kindness.

F

Factory Farm   Recurring problems, circular events, crowded bars
and bedrooms haunted by ghosts.

Failure to Climax During Telephone Sex
Your life will be full of difficulties.

Fake Rolex   The watch looks good but its weight gives it away
and after a while the gold colour starts to chip
away, leaving a metal that looks like it might be
steel or aluminium. The dream portends insincerity
from friends, exploitation from workmates, and
duplicity from children.

If the fake Rolex is **running backwards** the
dream signifies a tight deadline which the dreamer
cannot possibly meet.

Fake Snow   To feel fake snow beneath your feet is a good
omen, predicting love in a pleasurable aspect or
money via an unexpected windfall.

Fake snow in your eyes is a negative sign,
standing as it does for hesitation, jealousy and
hardship caused by extravagance.

If fake snow **covers the garden and the rooftops
turning the whole landscape into something akin to
a Yuletide department store window** you will be
married, and sooner than expected.

Falling Through the Poverty Trap
A common Modern Dream.

If you **tumble down and down in the dark,
falling so far and landing so badly that you break
your back and both legs and cannot get up again**
the dream stands for untold riches, success beyond
your wildest imaginings.

False Politeness of a Drunken Thug on a Train

If the thug says 'Ladies first' the dream warns of an assault.

If he has a **tattoo of a spider all across his face** the dream signifies mysterious obstacles.

If he **belches loudly and then says 'pardon'** the dream predicts a long argument with a close friend.

If he **stinks of nicotine, booze, piss or glue** the dream foretells of a rail crash, chopper down or maritime disaster.

Fan Club

To dream of **joining** a fan club augurs wealth and success.

To dream of **running** a fan club augurs ill, whilst a dream of **being expelled** from a fan club foretells a future of friendships and great happiness.

Far Right Victory in Free and Fair Elections

People will get what they deserve.

Fashion Café

Unhappiness, trouble with taxes, confusion about prices.

Faster-than-Light Travel

A dream of stasis, entrapment, stillness.

Fatherhood by Sperm Donation

Distance in love, or the doubling of doubt.

Father's Face in a Rorschach Test

Modern Dreams are nothing if not self-conscious, littered as they are with the props and apparatus of psychological and psychiatric testing and interpretation. The dream of a Rorschach Test has a common meaning that you will be prone to clumsiness in the days ahead, especially when carrying liquids.

To dream of seeing your own father's face in the pattern of a Rorschach Test depends for its meaning on the expression of the patriarch. If he is **smiling** you will have good fortune, if he is **frowning** you will have an enjoyable sexual

encounter, whilst if his expression is **ambivalent or confused** you will face a period of serious illness.
See also **Flash Cards (PSI Testing)**

Fax Machine   Loneliness by night.

If the fax **uses plain paper** the dream tends more to the positive, if it **uses dedicated fax paper** it tends more to the negative.

A dream of **receiving a fax which has a thick black line all the way down both sides, rendering large portions of the text unreadable**, it is a bad omen for those who work at night.
See also **Dirty Faxes**

Feeling that Life is Unreal

Words and actions by your colleagues and friends seem to lack meaning, the scenes are blurred and fogged, scenery and audio are distant. This classic Modern Dream plays often in the re-run cinema of sleep. If dreamt by an adult it signifies the offer of a part in a theatrical production, film or television series. If dreamt by a child it signifies that the week ahead will be one of difficulty and change.

Feet Stuck in Quick-Drying Cement

If the dreamer's feet have been **encased by accident** the dream foretells a double wedding.

If the feet have been **encased deliberately** (as a prank or as a punishment by organised criminals) it predicts a competition, election or other contest.

Fight in a Kebab Shop

Daily accidents and banal trials such as blown fuses, bent keys, laddered tights and broken heels await the dreamer.

Figure You are Hunting through the Corridors of Doom Bears Your Own Face   Like other dreams of self-harm this dream casts doubts about your motives or plans.

To **catch and kill** the figure which bears your own face in Doom stands for success in assuaging these doubts.

To **lose your quarry** and get lost, blundering

through the grey-green corridors alone, shooting
only at shadows, indicates a future of apprehension
and uncertainty.

File has a Damaged Resource Fork

To dream of a file with a damaged resource fork
signifies melancholy to those who are most often
cheerful and a month of enforced sobriety to those
who are normally drunk.

Finger in the End of a Shotgun

A villain points a shotgun at the dreamer who, in
some illogic of self-preservation, calmly sticks his
or her finger in the barrel of the gun. There is eye
contact. The contact is maintained. The villain
pulls the trigger on the blocked gun which swells,
swells and then bursts backwards, exploding,
singeing the villain, turning his hair upwards, his
face and clothes black, a cloud of soot hanging
thickly in the air. The dream warns of a sexual
relationship in which the power is not where it first
seemed to be.

See also **Cartoon** *and* **Mickey Mouse**

Fingers Caught in a Food Blender

If a young woman dreams that her fingers are
caught in a food blender then she will be beset by
many suitors; if she is **married** her life will be filled
with many beautiful and healthy children. For an
older woman the same dream means that she will
soon enter the menopause and for a **man** the dream
foretells of an unpleasant sexual experience.

Fingers Trapped in an Escalator

This dream indicates serious troubles in the days
ahead.

Fingerprinting a Family Member

The dream commonly involves the fingerprinting
of your children, spouse or grandparents.

If the fingerprints show **whirls** you will make a
wise investment; if they show **spirals** you will fall
in love.

If the fingerprints taken are **blurred** the dream foretells an accident.

If **threats or force must be used** in the taking of the fingerprints the dream will be followed by strife.

To dream that **your own fingerprints are taken** foretells that a close friend will break a promise.

Fingertip Search The dreamer finds him or herself outdoors, on hands and knees, placed shoulder to shoulder amongst a long, long line of people, some police, the rest volunteers. The line advances slowly but surely, picking over some rough and broken terrain as the people map the ground before them with their fingers, searching for items which may be either rubbish or clues to some terrible crime.

If the dreamer finds **sweet wrappers** the dream tells of happiness ahead.

If the dreamer finds **condoms, jewellery** or **photographs** the dream predicts romance.

If the dreamer finds **items which cannot be recognised** (weather worn, fragmented, broken or simply mysterious, impossible, unknowable) the dream predicts a horrible loss or painful death for a friend or close relation.

Fire Extinguisher If the extinguisher is filled with **water** you will make new friends.

If it is filled with **foam** you will make enemies.

Fire Proof Curtains

Economies caused by planning, diversions created by love, unhappiness caused by memories.

Firewall The firewall, mainstay of protection for computer networks, is a powerful symbol in Modern Dreams.

To dream **the construction of a firewall** predicts a dispute with neighbours.

To dream that **a firewall has been penetrated** predicts an illness in the family, particularly for those with children.

Fish Fingers   A common dream concerning the family, each fish finger denoting the birth of a child.

If the fish fingers are a **well-known brand** you will be happy.

If they are a **supermarket's own range** or that of an **obscure bulk-produce store** you will suffer hardships and unhappiness.

To dream of fish fingers **covered in ketchup** augurs ill for those in finance or manual labour.

Fitted Carpets   A warning of struggles and troubles forgotten or repressed.

If the carpets have **bubbles, bumps** or **other irregularities** there will be tension in a place of work.

A fitted carpet that is **worn** portends fighting in a bar or dissent in a place of worship.

Flash Cards (PSI Testing)

Self-conscious Modern Dreams are filled with the paraphernalia of psychological testing and interpretation.

If you dream of the flash cards **commonly used in experiments on Telepathic Communication** – circle, square, wave, triangle – in an institutional setting (bare concrete room with observation window, bare table, shuttered windows) you are being warned of a period of loneliness.

If you dream of such flash cards **in the context of a domestic setting** – e.g. a kitchen table, surrounded by the props and scenery of blissful daily life – you will be happy.

To dream that **someone sends you the image of the wave card** foretells of a journey to the sea.

A dream of **being in analysis** is a prediction of domestic affairs in turmoil, new or replacement furniture or a successful venture into a new part of town.

If the dream involves **group therapy** it predicts solitude.

If the dream involves **art therapy** it predicts

84

compromise in business, ingratitude in family and clumsiness in a car, shed or garden.

See also **Father's Face in a Rorschach Test**

Flavoured Condoms

To dream of these bright and tasty contraceptives predicts new experiences, new musical trends or new political solutions.

If the **taste of the contraceptives makes one feel sick** the dream predicts a period of solitude or risk in business.

Flight Path

Jealousy and discontentment will come to he or she who dreams of **living beneath** a flight path.

A dream of **planning flight paths** drawing lines between the cities, countries and continents of the world is a sign of restlessness.

Flip-Flops

The cheap semi-disposable rubber or plastic footwear known as the flip-flop is a symbol of fickleness or a warning of a friend with an easily swayed heart or an easily persuaded mind.

Flock Of Ravens Morphing Into a Dog

You will die a hopeless and degrading death.

Floodlights

A friend will offer you a new insight or perspective on an important aspect of your life.

Flotation Tank

A situation reversed. A daytime appointment doubled in length or significance.

Fluorescent Light

A flickering light predicts changes to your travel plans.

If the light is **glimpsed at night in a building far away** (a high-rise or office block) the delays will be serious.

To dream of **a job interview** in a room lit only by a single, flickering fluorescent light is to foresee bad fortune for your children.

Flying Long Haul

A dream of hard work, ardour, complex transactions of a financial kind.

Flynt, Larry

The outspoken paraplegic pornographer is a symbol of free speech when he appears in a dream.
See also **Golden Wheelchair**

Foam Party

You will contract an infection if you attend a foam party in a dream.
See also **Breakdancing** *and* **Discothèque**

Food Aid

A generous gift from a relative is on the cards. If **shoving and pushing starts as the food aid arrives on lorries** in a dream the gift will have to be divided with relatives or friends.

Format Battle

To dream of a battle to secure market share between alike but rivalrous technological formats (such as that which took place between direct and alternating current or between VHS and Beta video tapes) predicts unruly behaviour in a son or daughter.

If the battle is **between rival formats of gaming consoles** (Mega Drive Vs Playstation Vs Nintendo etc.) the unruly behaviour will be that of a parent or grandparent.

Former Miss Washington

A former Miss Washington in a dream stands for pleasure beyond the dreamer's wildest imaginings.

Former Soviet Union

To dream of the doomed former Soviet Union is to dream that your enemies will ensnare you.

Temptations from outside your neighbourhood will divide your family, whilst tension within the home itself will cause unhappiness, mismanagement, inadequate systems of health care, bad communication and poor planning, as well as a rise in crime and a shortage of luxury goods. Religion will prosper.

Formica

The popular and resilient work-surface has proved a significant presence in many Modern Dreams, especially in its patterned forms, not so much an element of kitchen furniture as a swirling landscape of coloured amoebic forms, the scale of which may vary enormously.

To dream that one is lost in a Formica landscape of this kind foretells of an unexpected death.

See also **Texture Dreams**

Four-Wheel Drive Control, ego aggrandisement, dangers and troubles ahead.

Fox, Michael J. You will be cunning, handsome, wily, resourceful and have a great smile.

Fragmented Hard Drive
Reckless behaviours, onerous responsibilities.

Frankenstein's Monster
A dream of self-loathing or self-doubt.

If the monster **sits alone weeping in some garage or outhouse** the doubts and loathing will fade.

If the monster is **pursued by townsfolk bearing torches** the dreamer will suffer an emotional setback.

Free and Fair Elections are Held for the First Time in Your House
The sudden appearance of posters and polling booths, outbreaks of sloganeering in the bedroom or at the breakfast table are all common features of this dream, which predicts an unsettling or total breakdown in family relations. In the days or weeks after this dream many spouses separate, children fight or turn against their parents and old or infirm members of a family are victimised.

Free Upgrade to Business Class
The dreamer will experience a problem of self-doubt or lack self-esteem.

Friendly Fire To dream that one is killed by friendly fire is a common and distressing Modern Dream in which one's death becomes an acrimonious bureaucratic tangle of lies and cover-ups, shambolic inquiries, accusations and paperwork. The dream is thus one of fear and the mistrust of authority, predicting

87

doubts and suspicions about the motive and aptitudes of one's supposed allies and friends.

If the dream is of **fire from the air** (friendly plane, mortar or rocket attack) it predicts a crisis of ethics or morality.

If the cause of one's death is **from the ground** (friendly land mine, hand grenade or machine gun ambush) the dream foretells of troubles with the fabric of a building, with health insurance or with money-saving schemes.

To **die alone** in a dream of friendly fire is a dream of great loneliness.

Frozen Yoghurt You will get a common cold.

Fruit Machine An abundance of bizarre variations on the gambling machines known as one-armed-bandits or fruit machines are found in the darkened bars and dimly-lit arcades and bars of Modern Dreamland.

To dream of **winning** by fruit machine is a relatively insignificant dream of subtle power loss and minor humiliation.

If the dream involves **feeding the money of an unknown other into the gaping mouth of a fruit machine** it stands for a victory in sport or politics, a personal gain in stature caused by action in word or in deed.

If the fruit machine in a dream stops at **three clenched fists** the dream predicts violence.

If it stops **at three open vaginas** it predicts a passionate sexual encounter, possibly with triplets.

Three staring eyes, three open mouths and **three bleeding palms** are all portents of bad luck.

If the fruit machine **starts its maximum payout,** kerchinking and kerchunking in that sound so very well beloved of us all, the coins flowing from the aluminium dispenser and spilling out onto stained carpets, then the dream predicts storms endured without shelter, cold winds and heavy rain.

88

F.T.S.E.   The streaming numbers of the F.T.S.E. index often appear in dreams.

If the numbers are **rising** the dream indicates that you will prosper against difficult odds.

If the F.T.S.E. numbers are **falling** you will suffer an embarrassment.

See also **Dow Jones, Hang Seng** *and* **Nikkei**

Fucking an Aerobics Instructor
You will engage in profitable work which will place you in an advantageous position.

See also **Fucking a Tennis Coach**

Fucking a Tennis Coach
The dream of fucking a tennis coach depends for its meaning on the location of the intercourse.

If it takes place **on the tennis court itself** you will have great happiness.

If it takes place **in the changing rooms or showers** you will be deserted.

If it takes place **in a car, garage or on a tiled patio** you will be unmasked, found out or discovered.

See also **Fucking an Aerobics Instructor**

Fucking the Bassist so you can Get Closer to the Saxophonist
The dream is a symbol of true love.

Fucking the Inflated Inside of a Wine Box
Common are the Modern Dreams in which the dreamer attempts intercourse with some new domestic item, purchase or appliance. Driven on by the late-capitalist project in which both the act of purchase and the products themselves are eroticised by design (organic, anthropomorphic, sensuous) and by marketing (erotic, aspirational) such dreams are the submerged backbone of the Modern Sexual Dreamscape.

For a man a dream of trying to fuck the inflated inside of a wine box is a sign of future progress, success, strength, health and intractability in the face of hardship.

89

For a woman the same dream is of failure, heartbreak and future disenchantment.

A dream in which a man finds himself fucking a tub of playdough, plastecine or other modelling substance, foretells of a period of loneliness or grief, whilst a dream of fucking the end of a vacuum cleaner tube indicates a crisis caused and made worse by the dreamer's own inadequacy. For a woman the same dream is a prediction of pleasure combined with fortune, health and happiness.

A dream of fucking oneself with a new brand of chocolate bar predicts success both in business and in leisure time, whilst a dream of pleasure gained by inserting a kitchen appliance, cleaning tool or plastic garden implement is an omen of hardship at work.

A dream in which the dreamer finds sexual pleasure by inserting an action man doll, Barbie doll or other action figure foretells of a birth.

Fun House

To dream of a fun house, with deceiving staircases, foreshortened walls and slanted ceilings, foretells of a change in your personal fortunes.

If the dream involves being forced to spend a night in the fun house, sleeping roughly and uneasily in its impossible bed the dream predicts that your child (or that of some close friend) will get ill.

G

Galaxians   To dream of Galaxians means that your friends will attack you.

Gameboy   Predicts a period of peace, composure, silence.

Games Arcade   To dream of the vast darkened interior space of a games arcade augurs ill for those intent on marriage or home-making.

To see one's **friend or lover** in this context – face illuminated by the flickering of many lights and LCD screens, spoken words submerged beneath the drone of so many virtual racetracks and battle zones – is to dream of new distance imposed by choice or by travel.

Gang Bang in the Back of a Transit Van

To dream of being gang-banged in the back of a transit van predicts great satisfaction of an intellectual kind.

If the van is merrily bouncing up and down on its springs the dream signifies a delirium of constant change.

If the dreamer **can't get it up** to take part in the gang bang the dream stands for stasis, problems surrounded by silence, ghosts and bad memories.

Gangsta Rap   The meaning of the dream depends on the source of the sound.

If **the music blares from a car as it passes** you will receive an unexpected windfall.

If **the car has stopped at some traffic lights** you will be faced with an unexpected tax demand.

A dream of **gangsta rap on a supermarket tannoy** predicts a conflict of interest.

Gap, The	Happiness, love from family, success in new enterprises.
Gas Mask	Dangers avoided by planning ahead.
Gates, Bill	A dream of the successful entrepreneur behind the Windows operating system and the Microsoft Corporation, Bill Gates, predicts a surfeit of leisure time. *See also* **Microsoft Company Picnic**

Gathering Aluminium Cans to Re-Sell at a Recycling Plant

The dreamer walks the streets with a large polythene bag finding beer cans, soda cans, Cola cans and Tango cans, each of which is picked up, drained of its residue and placed in the bag.

If the dream features **a good crop of collected cans** it bodes well for travel plans and arrangements regarding houses or gardens.

If the pickings of aluminium are **meagre** the dreamer will face a depression.

Geeks	A dream of bad-skinned geeks, lacking in social skills, indolent, unwashed and surrounded by half-drunk sodas and half-eaten pizza is a dangerous dream whose meaning is revealed in the details of their actions.

If the geeks are **laughing** you and your children are in danger.

If the geeks are **making out on a sofa** your recent investments in property have been unwise.

If the geeks are **surfing the web, watching TV** or **trying out a new brand of junk food** your health will deteriorate rapidly.

Worst of all dreams of geeks is that of **a lone geek wandering aimlessly in a city or town.** Like **Yardies** in this respect the geeks have no meaning except as agents of connection, in this case purely negative. Geeks connect symbols as they walk, spreading disaster as they go. A geek that drifts from a **shoe store to a travel agent** means you will find yourself forced to travel on foot. A geek that glances from a mini-mall fountain to a flooring specialist means that your house will suffer leaks and flooding. A dream that a geek passes you directly after passing a funeral parlour indicates a certain death.

See also **Yardies** and **Rastafarian**

Geiger Counter   Sleepless nights, speeches from strangers, whispering from friends.

General Anaesthetic

This dream of Modern oblivion takes its meaning from the immobility induced in the subject, reflecting as it does, the dreamer's need for stability, stasis and security.

A dream in which **the dreamer is placed under general anaesthetic by a member of his or her family** has the opposite meaning, inferring a strong desire to escape their restrictions.

Getting Married in Disneyland

This dream means that you will suffer great pain and misfortune by the revelation of secrets.

Getting Married Underwater

The significance depends on the *temperature* and *condition* of the water.

If the water is **warm and clear** it is a good omen, especially for those who work in food management or preparation.

If the water is **cold** or **cloudy** it augurs less well for the future.

Ghettoes   You will be poor.

See also **Sink Estates**

Ghost Message on the Answering Machine

With its penchant for distortion, inaudible voices and truncated narrative the answering machine provides a powerful symbolic locus for many Modern Dreams. To dream of messages left by the dead is common enough and suggests that the dreamer has neglected important obligations.

The dream of a message truncated at a vital point reveals that a plot may be hatched against you, whilst a message in gibberish means a child (or other relation) would like to speak to you.

A dream in which the telephone cable connected to an answerphone is plugged directly into the earth is a sign that you have unfinished business with the dead.

See also Tape Jammed or Tangled, Audio Tape Tangled in the Branches of a Tree *and* Strange Breathing on the Entryphone

Ghost-writer
To dream that you are a ghost-writer is an ill omen for your work or business plans.

If the dream involves your writing on behalf of a sporting personality its meaning is reversed.

To dream that your own life story is being written by a ghost-writer augurs well for your future.

Giving Birth to Consumer Durables
White goods, electronic devices and photographic equipment are commonly the subject of such dreams in which items of everyday technology are ejected from the body as in a difficult labour. For the most part these dreams are unimportant, indicating only minor changes in one's domestic affairs.

The dream of giving birth to two paracetamol tablets is of more concern, indicating as it does a forthcoming catastrophe.

The dream of giving birth to training shoes is a prediction of danger and flight.

Glasses Fixed with Elastoplast
The dreamer will be helped to understand a problem by a friend.

Global Warming
To dream of global warming is a premonition of tears.

If the polar ice caps are melting the tears will be great whilst if the cities of man are devastated and

94

flooded and if **unnatural storms lash the earth** the tears will be violent.

A dream that **one takes refuge in a tall, tall building to escape the rising waters** of the global catastrophe has no meaning in a dream unless one is accompanied by a child – in this instance the dream foretells of pregnancy or promotion.

A related dream is that of a **second ice age.** In this Modern Dream one finds oneself in a world turned brittle, white and intemperate – the roads are sheets of dark glass, the skies grey, the trees, pylons and fountains delicate sculptures of frost. To **break the ice** in this situation stands for change or danger, whilst **finding footprints in a field of fresh snow** indicates a meeting, a death or a need for new direction in one's life.

Glue Sniffing	Trust to chance and intuition.
God	*See* **Scientists have Taken a Photograph of God**
Golden Limousine	Pleasure, boundless and beyond reason.

Golden Wheelchair

To dream of a golden wheelchair, as used by the outspoken paraplegic pornographer Larry Flynt, is a dream of success and happiness achieved at great cost.
See also **Flynt, Larry**

Gothic Punks

If the Goths are **boys** the dream predicts happiness with true friends.

If they are **girls** it portends deceit.
See also **Skinheads**

Graceland

The fine white Memphis mansion in which Elvis Presley spent his final years of decadence, obesity and depravity foretells the opposite – a time of simple and healthy domestic bliss.

If the **gardens of Graceland are permeated with the smell of a barbecue or a cook-out** there will be a visit from neighbours, news from strangers or a birth in the family.

Graffiti Bears Your Phone Number

To dream your own phone number written in graffiti on the walls of a toilet foretells the discovery of an error in the work you have most recently completed.

If the number is written in **felt pen** the error could be advantageous.

If the number is **scratched into the paintwork** the error could prove problematic.

Graveyard of Torn-Down Statues

The dreamer finds him or herself in a graveyard of monuments and statues depicting the heroes, ideals and leaders of a former era, now deposed and discredited.

To dream of **a wander amongst these toppled leaders, lying in rows of undignified piles, broken, often limbless and rusting,** warns the dreamer of a disagreement with a close friend.

If **the toppled statues are largely of Stalin** the disagreement will be serious and will have unpleasant consequences for the dreamer.

A related dream which also involves the humbling of the great and the powerful is that in which the dreamer is in a **mob intent on burning records and other merchandise relating to such discredited or scandalous musicians as Elvis Presley, Niggers With Attitude or The Beatles.** To see idols burn in this way, the flames consuming promotional photographs, album covers and picture T-shirts alike in an atmosphere of ugly hatred foretells that false hopes will mislead the dreamer, deceiving and abusing, until he or she is left in a whirlpool of despondency.

See also **Stalin, Joseph**

Grebos   *See* **Hell's Angels**

Groupies   Groupies are symbols of raw and unlicensed desire. The more groupies there are the greater the desire and the more wanton it may be.

A dream of **picking out which groupies you want**

to fuck from the front row of a concert predicts
difficult decisions in the days or weeks ahead.

To dream of **having to wait outside the tour bus
while the bassist is getting a blow job from a
groupie** predicts frustration, jealousy and mistrust.

The dream of **sharing groupies** foretells trouble.
If you are sharing groupies with the **roadies** the
trouble will be serious.

To dream of **being a groupie,** hanging around
the stage door of rock venues in the hope of getting
some action predicts a life of freedom and great
pleasure unfettered by convention.

See also **Hoodlums, Hooligans** *and* **Roadies**

Gucci Bag   Big problems from small things.

Guggenheim (Bilbao)

The popular face of touristic post-modernism
stands for domestic problems caused by neglect of
property.

H

Hair Extensions   Insecurity at work, in the bedroom and in solitude.

Hall of Mirrors   To dream of a hall of mirrors is to foresee a period of rest and relaxation.

If the reflections are **amusing** the time off will be productive.

If they are **disturbing** it will be unpleasant and damaging.

See also **Mirror Ball** *and* **Discothèque**

Hand Jive   The tight, repetitive and formalised movements of the hand jive encode a message for the dreamer spelled out letter by letter. Thumbs up is the letter 'a', thumbs down is 'b', thumbs pointed together is 'c'. Fist clenched upwards is a 'd', fist clenched downwards is an 'e', etc. For a full breakdown of the **Hand Jive Alphabet** and related topics see the excellent *Coded Communication in Dreams*, Kavannagh, Hume, Davies et al, Sleep Press, 1998.

Hands Made of the Silver Flowing and Transforming Stuff like the Bad Android from 'Terminator'

A change of heart or stubbornness of mind.

Hang Seng   The Korean Market's Share Index is exceptionally volatile. Those who dream of it are being warned to be wary of their own tempers or those of their companions.

See also **Dow Jones, F.T.S.E.** *and* **Nikkei**

Happy Hour   Comprising cheap drinks in a more or less empty bar, the dream is of illness for a friend or family member. The dreamer will spend long hours tending someone at their bedside.

If there is a **special promotion on Vodka/Red**

Bull or **Margheritas** the dream predicts a long night of emotional conversation.

Hat with a Plastic Dick on top of it, the Front of the Hat Bearing the Slogan 'DICKHEAD'

The meaning of the dream lies in the angle of the plastic penis.

If it is **erect** the dreamer will have good and happy life.

If it is **limp** the dreamer will be tempted by evil.

Haunted Night Club

A dream of a haunted night club predicts problems in the present arising from persons in your past.

If the ghost is that of **a DJ who plays slow tunes to an empty dancefloor** the problems will involve an ex-lover.

If the ghost is **a poltergeist throwing glasses to the ground or cloakroom tickets in showers through the air** you will find plans ruined by unexpected arrivals, changes of heart and inclement weather.

Having Sex in a Power Cut

Hopes frustrated or dashed, expectations unmet.

Hawaiian Shirt

If the shirt has a **lurid floral pattern** you will get money from an undisclosed source.

If it has a pattern of **beautiful fluttering humming birds** a threat will be made to your life or your livelihood.

Hawking, Steven

If Hawking is **silent** the dream bodes ill, whilst if he is **speaking** the dream bodes well.

Hawn, Goldie

The buxom blonde bombshell stands for great riches when she features in a dream.

Health Insurance

A dream that warns of its opposite – danger, illness and medical problems.

Hearst, Patty

A dream of the heiress turned kidnap-victim turned revolutionary terrorist turned movie star and socialite predicts danger, or happiness through a change in career.

Heart Transplant The dream depends for its meaning on the identity of the donor.

If it is a **stranger** the dream suggests a secret passion or unfulfilled desire.

If it is a **spouse or other family member** the dream suggests a conflict of interest, fight, spat or argument about duties.

If the donor heart comes from a **member of the opposite sex** or from **someone of another race** the dream stands for confusion and turmoil. Few dreamers find contentment in the week following such a dream.

To dream that **you are watching your own heart transplant operation,** staring down at your body reduced to a blood soaked cabinet of ribs and organs surrounded by surgeons, or glimpsing the scene in mirrors and monitors, signifies the need for a serious rethink in your life. It is important to slow down and take time to consider all your options.

Held Aloft by King Kong

The mighty gorilla King Kong symbolises the power of animatronics, and to dream of him means that you will have a suitor who works in special effects.

The dream of **being held aloft by King Kong** is especially fortuitous because it means that the suitor will be a good lover.

Hell's Angels You can expect trouble if these outlaw bikers roar into the city, town, village or neighbourhood of your dreams.

If the Hell's Angels are **smiling** the trouble will be large.

If the Hell's Angels are **called Dave, Skull, Chip, Twig, Mr Max** and **Mender** you will probably escape with your life.

101

Helpline

Sorrow, tight and intently focused, will come to those who call a **software support helpline** in a dream.

If the dream is of a call to **the Samaritans** or other **telephone counselling service** joy and friendship are predicted, the length of the friendship determined by the length of the call.

A dream in which **one calls a telephone helpline but the phone keeps ringing and ringing and no one answers** foretells of a period of silence between friends, planned absence between lovers and a holiday from work.

Helter Skelter

To dream that one is **descending** on a helter skelter ride foretells a change in one's employment circumstances.

To **see the words helter skelter written down** in a dream is to foresee bloodshed of a dramatic and most unpleasant kind.

Hep Cats

Conflict of interests, confusion of intentions, crises caused by money or additional work.

Hi-Jacking

The long, testing hours ensconced in the belly of a 747, living off hostage-food, sweating, ill and suffering cramps symbolise childbirth, long struggles, court cases and bitter divorce.

If there are **hysterical children** on the plane you will lose a close friend due to rivalry in love.

For every **corpse thrown blindfold from the doorway to the runway below** expect six more months of bad luck, enforced celibacy and sleeplessness.

If **passengers, captain or crew make a foolhardy bid for freedom** expect a public disgrace before family and friends.

If the dream is of a hi-jacked plane which **gets blown up on the runway,** the whole thing turning into a huge fireball, the prediction is of good news arriving by post, travel at night and sudden inspiration regarding a difficult task.

102

Hippies A dream of hippies with long hair and flowers portends a conflict solved by violence.

If the hippies are **stoned** the dream augurs badly for business and ventures in commerce.

A dream of **sleeping** hippies is a dream portending a violent betrayal.

History Repeating Itself

This common Modern Dream foretells of success in love or honourable progress in school education.

Hitch-Hiking In the most common dream of hitch-hiking the Modern Dreamer waits by a roadside and no cars pass. Rain begins to fall. The dream, most often taking place in the dead of night, speaks of a decision waiting to be made, or of a secret waiting to be told.

If **graffiti on some sign at the roadside bears the dreamer's name** the next week will involve a meeting with a kindred spirit.

If the dreamer does receive a lift the meaning is determined by the nature of the intimate encounter in the enforced privacy of the cab.

If **the driver is a racist who can't keep his opinions to himself** the dream predicts a problem solved by violence.

If **the driver won't take his hands off the dreamer's knee** the dream foretells of friction at work, happiness at home.

If the driver is **an ex-con just out of prison** or an **ex-squaddie just out of the army** the dream predicts a period of discipline, especially if the conversation turns to gun control, law and order or 'the problem with Northern Ireland'.

A dream of hitch-hiking in which **the dreamer receives a lift from a close friend or family member** is a warning of frayed tempers, promises broken and troubles arising from inadequate plans.

A **ride in silence** stands for loneliness. The longer the silence, broken only by road-noise and the clack-clack-clack of the windscreen wipers, the longer the loneliness will last.

Holder, Noddy To dream of the lead singer of the glam rock band Slade predicts an outbreak of laddish behaviour.

If Noddy is **wearing platforms** the behaviour will be especially oafish and regrettable.

See also **Platform Shoes**

Holding a Hand-Grenade with the Pin Pulled Out for as Long as You Dare just to Prove that you can do it, Eyes Closed in the Bathroom, the Blood Beating in Your Ears

The dream is a complaint from deep in the psyche. The dreamer's life is turgid, static, boring – change is needed. If there is no change there will be violence.

Holding a Lighter or Mobile Phone Aloft at a Rock Concert

You will be a hero, if only for a brief moment in time.

See also **Mobile Phone Set to an Embarrassing Ring** *and* **Impressed by a Tribute Band**

Holiday Camp These bleak and already charmless recreational institutions, with their pastel coloured chalets, games rooms, discotheques and miles of bland sandy beaches, are symbols of strengths in a marriage but of deep divisions in a family.

Holiday Resort You will be blessed with a gift for new languages.

See also **Hotel is Still Under Construction**

Home Movie Has Unwittingly Captured a Historical Event

See **Zapruder Dream**

Homeless People Homeless people are everywhere in Modern Dreams, littering doorways, pissing here and there, foraging for food and for aluminium cans which can be recycled.

One homeless person stands for debts and financial hardships. **Two** homeless people stand for bankruptcy. **Three** homeless people predict that your feelings will be hurt by the actions of a close friend. **More than three** homeless people signify spite and trouble caused by reckless behaviour.

If the homeless people have **gathered around a fire on some derelict area of ground** they symbolise the family, for the importance of blood ties and mutual support.

If the homeless people are **dead** (curled foetal in a cardboard box, floating face down in the canal, slabbed out on a table in a morgue) they symbolise boundless wealth to come.

See also **Sleeping in a Doorway Under Cardboard Boxes**

Honda Goldwing Mistrust, hurt caused by impudence, stasis.

Hood Ornament The dream depends for its meaning on the type of ornament.

To dream of **the winged silver female form seen atop Rolls Royce cars** predicts flight from danger and towards love, happiness and security.

To dream of **the bisected wheel of the BMW logo** predicts divisions in a household or a nation, dilemmas in a marriage or a business organisation.

See also **Groupies, Hoodlums** *and* **Roadies**

Hooded Sweatshirt

The need to escape. The hooded sweatshirt is a modern womb in which to hide; the darkness and enforced privacy of the hood itself signifies fear and inability to cope.

To dream that **one receives a hooded sweatshirt as a present** is a dream of a love that will be ended in haste.

Hoodlums Hoodlums are symbols of our untamed desires. Hanging about on the street corners of many Modern Dreams, chewing gum, slicking back their hair, flicking their flick-knives and wolf-whistling at defenceless young women, they are warning the dreamer that the balance between order and chaos is a tentative, ephemeral one.

105

To dream of **sleeping** hoodlums is to foresee a maritime disaster.

A dream of hoodlums who are **held behind bars** foretells of a period of uneasy peace, the calm before a storm.

A dream of **dead** hoodlums predicts wealth, gained by suspect or illegal means.

See also **Hooligans, Groupies** *and* **Roadies**

Hooligans   The dream of **Hooligans** is similar to that of **Hoodlums** only more powerful, since the Hooligan is the more dangerous and anarchic force in a dream, as in life. The hooligan with his lager-can, half-brick and shoulders draped in a national flag, suggests an inescapable breakdown in the balance between order and chaos.

To dream of hooligans **causing trouble on a crowded train** predicts a frustration of your social ambitions.

See also **Groupies, Hoodlums** *and* **Roadies**

Hopper, Dennis   The appearance of Dennis Hopper in a dream foretells of a problem with trust or understanding.

If the star is **wearing shades** it augurs instead for success in matters creative and compassionate.

Hormone Injections

Success achieved by the intervention of a powerful friend.

Hospital Corridors   Archetypes of deep fear and psychic unease these maze-like, scuffed-white and fluorescent-lit passageways, with their ubiquity of complex and misleading signage, provide the setting for many Modern Dreams.

To dream that one is **lost** in this context is the commonest dream of all and signifies bad news, especially for fishermen, sculptors and market analysts.

To dream of **pursuit** through such hospital corridors can signify many things depending largely on the identity of the pursuer. To be chased by a

106

doctor or other medical professional predicts success in any forthcoming tests. Pursuit by a **fellow patient** predicts failure. Pursuit by a **blonde nurse from the migraine unit** signifies failure in love.

There are some who dream that they find a door in such hospital corridors, **an unmarked door of mysterious purpose, and that entering the space behind this door they hear the most beautiful music.** The dream has but a slight meaning, foretelling as it does of a minor injury or accident resulting in a graze.

Doubtless the worst dream of a hospital corridor is to **find oneself aboard a gurney or medical trolley, making smooth and speedy progress down these passageways, unable to move, eyes locked upwards on the strafing strip-lights embedded in the ceilings.** This dream predicts an onset of blindness or the rapid arrival of unexpected news.

Hospitality Suite Dreaming of the backstage hospitality suite at a TV chat show augurs well for those planning or organising parties, wedding receptions, christenings, work outings and the like.

If there are **drunken celebrities** in the suite you will struggle with a task, finding distractions where focus, graft and application are needed.

If the **celebrities are throwing twiglets, hula hoops and other snacks at each other** the dream predicts a welcome from an old acquaintance who has, until now, been indifferent to the dreamer.

Hostile Take-Over of One's Family

To dream that one's family is subject to a take-over by a hostile corporation or business interest is an omen of change. One will move house, switch jobs or even emigrate in the months following this dream.

The broader genre of the dream is that in which the family is mistakenly treated as a business or like institution. If **corporate accountants present their offer at a breakfast or brunch meeting in the family** kitchen the dream predicts a marriage founded not on love but on money and social position.

A related dream is that in which one's family residence undergoes a rigorous inspection by officials concerned with health and safety in the workplace. Toothbrushes, carpets, kitchen surfaces, stairwells, doors and cupboards are all examined and the family members are quizzed in isolation about techniques and procedures for health and safety. The dream denotes doubt in the heart and hesitation in the mind.

Hotel Soap
To dream of hotel soap is a reminder of the transitory and ephemeral nature of all things. It may indicate the end of a job, a relationship or even, in extreme cases, the end of a life.

To dream of **stealing** hotel soap suggests deceit.

Hotel is Still Under Construction
You arrive at reception, weary after long hours of travel, to find the carpets covered in polythene sheeting and ductboards, a film of dust on every surface and the constant din and noise of construction work filling the air like a mighty battle of olden times.

If the room you are allocated has a direct view down onto the deep and noisy pit of open foundations the dream signifies that an investigation into your past is on the cards.

If the drilling, hammering and banging begins at precisely 6am it signifies an early retirement with plentiful bonuses.

To dream that you hear the noise of constant drilling but cannot locate the source is a common Modern Dream whose meaning has been very much debated. You may wander the corridors for hours, barefoot and sleepless, ears sensitised to the rise and fall of the hideous din, the relentless pounding of steel against concrete. No matter which way you turn you will never get closer to the sound, which always seems to be coming from 'just over there'. The true meaning of the dream lies in the persistence and method that you employ to try to find the source of the noise and cacophony. If you **enlist the help of other residents** the dream foretells of a successful marriage or business venture; if you **complain to the night porter,** or **demand that the duty manager be woken from his slumber to explain or further investigate**, the dream foretells that a confidence will be broken. Finally, if you search **alone** the dream betokens a death from fire, cold or drowning.

See also **Holiday Camp** *and* **Holiday Resort**

Hot-Wiring a Car Short tempers, emotional scenes.

House is Made of Plasticine

Common are the Modern Dreams in which the substances of daily reality are substituted or transformed. The most common of such is the dream that one returns home to find that one's house or apartment is made of the popular modelling material called Plasticine. Entering one's abode one fears to touch the walls, floor, or furniture in case of puncture, breaking, or leaving marks. The dream foretells of a period of indecision and a failure to carry out one's plans.

Hula Hoops Repetition at work, return to harmony, origins and starting points, seduction by circular arguments.

Human Shield To dream that one is held as part of a human shield augurs ill for one's career.

If one's **captors are ill-tempered and abusive** the meaning of the dream is reversed.

I

I Can't Believe It's Not Butter

The best butter substitute on the market has only slight meaning in a dream, predicting small changes in status or in the forthcoming weather.

See also **Vaginal Deodorant**

I.D. Parade/Police Line-up

Presence in a dream line-up indicates a desire to be recognised. It may suggest a career in show business or in politics, or an act of self-revelation or exposure.

To dream that one is **picked out** during an I.D. Parade foretells of a holiday romance.

Ikea

Ikea, the giant of Swedish home-assembly furniture with a business empire that spans three continents, foretells a new chance for old people, projects or ideas.

'Imagine' by John Lennon Sung and Played Badly by a Drunken semi-pro Wrestler in his early 20s, Slumped at a Baby Grand Piano in the Lobby of a Holiday Inn, Columbus, Ohio, during a Spring Snowstorm as Armed Guards Check I.D. on the Entrances to Elevators and Other Wrestlers gather closely round, Beers in Hand and Tears in their Eyes

The dream is one predicting sadness.

If **the song ends before a fight starts** there will be a revolution.

Imported Lager Change going back on itself, a prediction of life lived in a pattern of loops, circles and waves.

Impressed by a Tribute Band or Solo Impersonator

To dream of attending a concert by a tribute band has no meaning in itself, but to dream that **one likes the band** has disturbing implications, largely of a medical nature.

111

Clapping a tribute band foretells an illness in the family.

Cheering or **whooping** foretells a death or maiming.

See also **Cover Version(s)**

Income Tax Returns

Laughter in a restaurant or bar, feigned clumsiness in the workplace, impotence in bed.

Incoming Wounded

Difficult choices and simple deceptions.

Incomprehensible DotCom Companies

The dream of incomprehensible DotComs is very common and implies little more than the return of a minor medical problem or the replay of some familiar marital argument.

In many such dreams the dreamer sees **advertisements for such DotComs in unlikely places** – projected onto pavements, skywritten by looping jet planes or scrawled as lewd graffiti in public toilets. In such dreams the prediction is of problems which will need to be solved urgently and with great resourcefulness.

To think that **the dreamer has a really brilliant idea for an internet start-up** foretells a long wrangle about money with parents or a child.

Industrial Action

For the lover dismay, for the traveller pause, for the child strength born solitude.

Industrial Estate

These nowheres of the Modern City feature often in dreams.

If you are **looking for a Unit that does not exist** you must be careful about who you let in on your carefully thought-out plans.

If **the signage is good** you should watch your back.

A dream in which **your car breaks down on the grey sliproad at the edge of an industrial estate** is an omen of troubles in politics, discouragement in business and losses in war.

112

Industrial Tribunal

To dream that one has to give evidence at an industrial tribunal portends a period of unnatural harmony in the home.

Inexperienced Barstaff Struggle with the Computerised Till in a Wine Bar

If there are **two** of them struggling the dream foretells of an accident that will have pleasant consequences.

If there are **three** of them struggling the dream predicts a month of restlessness at work and in the heart.

If all work in the bar stops as each member of staff gives their opinion, tries out their plastic 'key' to log-on at the till and their formula for cancelling an item, or securing change for the cigarette machine (or whatever) the dream portends a change to more inclement weather.

A dream in which the bar staff in question **blush or start to stammer at the problems arising from the computerised till, withdrawing any eye contact previously made** foretells of a problem with a daughter or son, or, for the childless, with the offspring of a friend or neighbour.

Inflatable Sex Doll To dream of sex toys is a complex and often cautionary business. In particular a dream of an inflatable sex doll most frequently means that the dreamer will be forced to tell lies in order to help out a friend.

The more **realistic orifices** the sex doll has, the more lies the dreamer will have to tell.

If **the doll has burst** it means there will be tears around the breakfast table.

If **the doll has evidently been used** (dripping semen, covered in sweat) it means there may be an unwanted pregnancy.

If the sex doll has **a cord to pull so that it speaks,** yelling: 'Yes. I like it like that.' Or 'Fuck me, fuck me harder,' the dream portends impotence, failure, rage.

113

A dream in which a sex doll is watching the
dreamer, blank eyes following, red mouth agape, is
an omen of misplaced trust.
See also Malfunctioning Sex-Aid

Inhaling the Air from Helium Balloons in order to Speak in High Voices
A dream predicting change.

If the participants in such pranksterish behaviour
are naked a disruption to train and other travel
services is predicted.

Instant Mashed Potato
Tenderness from unexpected quarters.

Insufficient Memory to Complete a Task
Ill health, especially breakdown, depression and
mental illness, will come to the dreamer.

Insulin Injection
Love at first sight.
See also Hormone injections

Insurance Scam
A dream of financing a holiday by reporting a
fictitious camera, make-up bag and wallet missing
from your baggage foretells a lie from someone
you trusted.

If the insurance company does not query your
claim the lie will be doubled, added to and
supported by others.

To dream of a bigger insurance scam (involving
the arson of a building or the sinking of an
unwanted ship) foretells of deceit by your children
or closest friends.

Internet Flirtation
You will be happy.

Internet Pornography with the People Removed
Your house will be unexpectedly empty for a
period of time.

Inter-railing
To dream of a youthful adventure, criss-crossing
Europe by train with not much more than a few
T-shirts and a rotten pair of training shoes, predicts
that you will be separated from a favoured friend.

If you meet **Scandinavians** the future will be rosy, if you meet **Germans** expect health problems.

Intimate Polaroids When memory cannot be trusted photographs are needed. To dream of polaroids taken during sexual intercourse is to doubt one's own memory – a sign of insecurity, weakness, even paranoia.

If the polaroids show **a partner** (or worse still, **an ex-partner**) the dreamer will soon come to doubt the true meaning of the relationship in question.

If the polaroids show **the dreamer him or herself** the doubts will concern other aspects of the dreamer's life.

A dream of polaroids **depicting oral sex** foretells of hunger, blight and famine.

Invented creatures A vast pantheon of invented creatures roam the diverse landscapes of Modern Dreams. Who has not dreamed of the Pokemon Picachu and Wartortle? Or of the Teletubbies LaLa and Po? Or of the frog Kermit and the swine Miss Piggy?

The meaning of these creatures is not so much in their actions as in their locations – to dream that **they visit you at home** predicts that you will receive many Valentine's cards; whilst to dream that they **turn up in your workplace** predicts troubles to come and a chance that you will be fired.

Of more concern are those dreams in which you **visit** such invented creatures **in their own natural habitat** – trading the 'real' world for the lime green hills of Tubbyland or the 2-D mazes and purple skies of Mewtwo's island. A dream of this kind suggests that you will be plunged, upon waking, into the deepest and most uncontrolled melancholy.

See also **Daleks**

Irish Theme Pub Calamity, dispute, conflicts, violence.

If there are **plastic shamrocks** the dream predicts the birth of healthy children.

If there are **fiddlers advertised** you will find yourself in an embarrassing position.

115

To dream of an Irish Theme Pub with a complex or contradictory national profile (e.g. it is called **Frankfurter Irish Keller and is run by some Moroccan guy called Ahmed and populated by a load of degenerate Swiss backpackers**) foretells of good fortune in business ventures.

See also **Themed Pub**

Ironic Shopping
To dream that one has returned from the shops with bags loaded with kitsch or ironic purchases predicts contentment in matters of the spirit.

Iron Lung
An iron lung is a symbol of life (breath, the soul) ruled by artifice and mechanics. The dream predicts entrapment, a life stifled by regulation and convention.

To dream that **one's own body is encased in an iron lung** is to foresee one's replacement in the workforce by some clever new technology or industrial process.

Ironing in Front of the TV
Love will be hidden by the day-to-day grind of living with another person.

Item of Foodstuff you have Selected is not Recognised by the Scanner and they have to Call over the Tannoy for the Guy to come and get a Price for It
A shaming dream. You will face humiliation from family, workmates or friends.

The greater the number of **impatient people** there are waiting behind you in the queue, the greater the humiliations to come.

Items Washed Up by the Ocean
Pollution, lawlessness and the pointed illogic of Modern Dreams have all played a part in the steadily increasing tide of detritus hurled upon the beaches of our contemporary subconscious. Driftwood, an old world symbol of compromise and surrender, has been replaced for the most part by **bubblewrap**, by **bleach**, **pop** and other plastic bottles as well as by **unrecognisable fragments of plastic in dulled yellow, orange, white and red**

116

whose function as a part of some toy, household device or garden implement has long since been rendered illegible/forgotten. Such **worn bottles, their logos erased and the shattered plastic fragments of hugely diverse size,** as driftwood before them, are symbols of the way time marks, changes and mellows us.

By contrast a dream of **finding condoms on the beach, whether washed up from the ocean or left there during the night,** is a prediction of new energy, new life, or mother/fatherhood by adoption.

Common are the dreams in **which unexpected or out-of-place items are found amongst the shoals of debris** described above. To dream of **a child's carseat washed up by the sea, its upholstery stripped, seat belts worn** is a dream of danger to your family, whilst a dream of **a child's 'realistic ray gun' beached upon the shore, its red plastic worn to a shimmer, its metal trigger snapped,** is a dream of travel and, in the worst case scenario, of suicide.

A dream of **beached bathroom cabinets, corners rounded and bruised, mirrors cracked or broken, their shipwrecked forms scattered on the beach like so many forlorn seals,** foretells of an unexpected period of rest and reflection, undertaken with reluctance but with ultimately self-preserving.

I.V.F.   Success in the organisation of parties, weddings and product launches.

J

James T. Kirk/William Shatner
To dream of this formidable and experienced
starship captain or his real-life counterpart, the
ageing actor from science fiction television **William
Shatner,** bodes well for those who wish to travel.
See also **Transporter Room**

Jargon
A man or a woman talking in jargon means the
dreamer should buy new furniture.

Jet Lag
Dreaming of jet lag is a sign that one's heart or
mind is elsewhere – the bored office worker, the
mother frustrated by her chores, the
night-watchman and the footballer held endlessly
in reserve all dream this dream.

If the jet lag is **accompanied by nausea** or even
hallucinations, the dream will be followed by travel
or by long distance phone calls.

Jet Ski
A dream which predicts failure brought about by
excessive pride.

Joined Places, Rooms, Objects and People
Design and architectural style in the world of
dreams normally follows leads, trends and
innovations established in the waking world.
However, in some instances it has been known to
take a bold and impressive step forward alone. The
example of **Joined Places, Rooms, Objects and
People** is one such case. If some locations in our
Modern world of dreams have found their best
description as being 'X but not X', (e.g. 'Paris but
not Paris') there are other locations and indeed
objects characterised by the formulation 'X but also
Y' or, to put it differently 'Y, but at the time Z'.

119

The resulting hybrid of dreamed cityscapes, buildings and objects may be mixtures of public and private spaces and/or of diverse functionalities, historical and national styles, further blurred by the conscious or unconscious distortions of memory, exaggeration and forgetting.

A dream set in some *joined place* (for example 'in the bedroom of my old house but in the reading room of Doncaster Public Library') is, at its heart, a dream of ambiguity, and indecision for the dreamer. The more places joined in the same dream location the greater the indecision predicted. A dream of being 'in a hotel at the seaside, only it's a private house in Coventry and that place I once ate in right next to the Empire State Building' thus signifies serious indecision.

Where *objects* rather than places are joined in a dream the subject may find him or herself holding, for example, a knife that later proves to be a torch, or searching for a key which is also a letter. Such dreamed objects of the joined class – knife/torch, key/letter, cup of coffee/DVD player – are unique to Modern Dreams and are capable of maintaining their ambiguous or double status for long periods of dream time, sometimes remaining forever undecided as to their true identity and sometimes shifting from one function to another as the dream itself appears to demand it.

A dream containing one or more *joined objects* foretells uncertainty, not on the part of the dreamer but on the part of those placed to judge, help or hinder him. The dream of *joined objects* is thus one of a significant moment of balance, crossroads or turning point in the dreamer's life where the future rests in the uncertain hands and judgement of others.

Finally there are Modern Dreams of *joined people*. In such pyrotechnically strange dreams there appear human figures and dream persons whose presence is double, as that of the *objects*

120

discussed above. A dream involving *joined people* is one of mistrust. The more such figures appear the greater the mistrust will be. If the joined person is a mixture of two people known to the dreamer (mother/sister or uncle/local shopkeeper) the dreamer will suffer at the hands of a loved one. If the dream involves a joining of **famous persons** (Harrison Ford/Gerald Ford or Madonna/Cher) the dreamer will suffer at the hands of a stranger.

See also **Negative Objects, Places and People** *and* **Unknown Electrical Goods**

Joint

If **you are rolling** the joint the dream bodes well. The bigger the joint the more good luck you will have.

If the dream is of a joint **that always seems to skip you as it circles the room** the meaning is reversed. The more times the joint passes you by the more ill fortune you will receive.

To dream of **smoking a joint but refusing to inhale** predicts a career in politics.

Joy Riders

Sallow-faced, shell-suited, high on glue, booze or simply adolescence, joy riders (like **Groupies**) are a symbol of desire unleashed in all its forms. To the lover they spell lust, to the money-man greed, to the gastronome avarice and gorging.

If the joy riders are **pursued hotly by the police** in a dream its meaning is reversed, standing as it does for a time of strict and fearful abstinence from all indulgence.

To dream of **a car crashed or simply abandoned** by joy riders, its doors open, radio still tuned to some pirate station, portends the flight of children from a family, an exodus of people, a change of job, heart or address.

Juggling Debts on a Series of Credit Cards

Your emotional commitments are too many and your resources and energies for dealing with them are too few. The dream warns that it is time to slow down and take stock, to sever those attachments which you can no longer justify.

Jukebox	A dream of a jukebox is a dream of anxieties concerning decisions already made.

If the jukebox seems to play its own choices regardless of whatever numbers you punch in the dream denotes bitter regret.

A dream of a CD jukebox, with an excessive profusion of choices, portends private confusion in a matter that is avowedly public.

Jump Cuts	A dream of jump cuts warns of dangers in everyday life.

If the jump cuts are interrupting the dialogue, rendering language as a series of unintelligible fragments, the dangers will come from close to home – from neighbours, family or even the dreamer him or herself.

See also Credits Sequence/End Titles

Junk Email	*See* Spam

Junk Mail	Common is the Modern Dream that one's house or apartment is deluged with junk mail. For the most part the dream augurs little more than the chance that strangers will alter one's life in a mischievous or light-hearted way.

If the junk mail is persistently addressed to a previous occupant, who has either moved on or deceased, the dream foretells that one will be mistaken for another in the context of business or romance.

If dream junk mail promises that one has been selected for a prize draw, that one has certainly won one of five hundred possible prizes and that one is possibly amongst the lucky six people who have won £250,000 then the dream predicts not riches but great happiness, in abundance and arising from true friendships.

Juvenile with Lip-Synching Problems

A host of young men with lip-synching problems walk the cold streets of Modern Dreams.
Pale-skinned, jittery and shadow-eyed, these youths are messengers from death, whose words and lip movements are rarely syncopated.

If one of these messengers **whispers directly in one's ear** a tragedy will not be averted in the next few days.

To dream that **one has been kissed** by a young man or young woman with lip-synching problems is to predict a terminated pregnancy, a hotel fire, or summer in a country never before visited.

See also **Groupies, Hoodlums, Hooligans** *and* **Roadies**

K

Kalashnikovs   Foreign travel, happiness at home.

Karan, Donna   Donna Karan is a symbol of new clarity and self-revelation.

Karaoke Lock-In   To dream of being trapped after-hours in a small and crowded basement karaoke bar is to foresee employment misfortune or an unhappy wedlock.

If **you are singing**, the dream may mean that travel to Japan is imminent.

To dream that **you are unable to follow the words on the karaoke machine** means that your life has become an incomprehensible and alienating routine. To **finish** the song in these circumstances, laughing gamely and 'giving it a go' is to accept your lot, most probably forever. To **leave the podium in anger or humiliation** is to allow the possibility of change.

A similar dream is that of staring in disbelief as **the dots, blips and scanning lines on an airport radar screen swim and blur in bewildering patterns.** This dream also contains the possibility for change. To **force the screen to focus**, regaining control and completing your job, indicates perseverance and future success. If you **fall into a trance**, unable to pull away from the seductive if disastrous spectacle of the radar screen, you will not get much further in life.

Kebab Half-Eaten and then Shoved into the Upturned Blower of a Hot-Air Hand-Dryer in the Gents' Toilets of a Barnsley Night Club, the Stench of Re-Cooking Meat Wafting on the Warm Air
    Murder, the incorrect apportioning of blame, beautiful language or rough sex.

125

Kensit, Patsy   Patsy Kensit, the well known rock-chick-about-town and girlfriend/wife of many rock-and-rollers is a symbol of survival, resilience and strength.

If Patsy is **wearing leather trousers** in the dream her meaning is reversed.

Ketamine   A dream of this powerful illegal hallucinogen foretells of a life-change, dark, profound and unexpected in direction.

Key Party   Swingers' parties of all kinds have often appeared in dreams, mostly signifying sexual frustration or unease in the dreamer.
See also **Wife Swapping**

Keys to a Locker at the Airport
The dream of finding the keys to a locker at the airport has its meaning in the great anticipation which characterises the dream. What will be in the locker? Will someone be watching it? How will your life change when the contents are collected? The dream means that you are approaching a crossroads in life and that decisions must be taken carefully.

If the locker has a 3 or a 5 or a 9 in its number the dream is unlucky and calls for caution.

If it has a **double 2** or better yet a **double 0** the dream signifies success and calls for bravery.

If you **open a locker for which you have found the key,** the meaning of the dream shifts to the significance of *what is found inside*. A dream in which one finds **money in unmarked bills** denotes unhappiness, whilst a dream of finding **gemstones** augurs well for those who would travel north. To find **guns** means love, to find **a bag stuffed with clothes** means change in the form of a new job or holiday, whilst finding a bag containing **blood-soaked limbs and body parts,** or **crudely severed heads,** foretells that you will be powerful.
See also **Suitcase Full of Cash**

126

Keystone Cops   The Keystone Cops are good omens in a dream, especially if the dreamer stands accused or on trial for some crime.

If these blundering comedians of law enforcement are **driving their station wagon and skidding on mud or on ice** the dream warns to beware a stranger, a message from a child or a figure in shadows.

If the Keystone Cops are **tripping up and getting into a fight** with each other the dream foretells of an end to heartbreak or a solution to some persistent problem at home or at work. Like other dreams involving seminal figures drawn from the world of silent comedy, a significant aspect of the dream is the silence with which the Keystone Cops endure all their sufferings, trials and tribulations. This aspect of the dream (and those of Buster Keaton, Charles Chaplin etc.) foretells that some forthcoming crisis will best be dealt with by stoicism, calm and a careful control on the dreamer's emotions.

Kid That Seems to Know Too Much

Such children haunt the streets, front rooms and playgrounds of many Modern Dreams. Already bored with death, well acquainted with perversity, sex and suffering, dull-eyed and apathetic in the face of a challenge, half-hearted even in watching TV, they augur well for the dreamer, whose own vitality and curiosity will rise in direct proportion to the blank indolence of the juveniles.

Kids have Tagged your Name All Around Town

To see your name tagged in luminous letters twenty feet high on the side of the railway tunnels, on the subway walls and on the trains themselves is a common Modern Dream in which these stylised textual echoes of oneself predict a time of doubts and confusions ahead. The more tags, the larger and more stylised they are the greater the doubts to come.

Worse yet is the dream in which you see a small and hyper-minimal tag – a refined squiggle made by the gesture of a pen not much greater than the flicker of a wrist – in the knowledge that this abstracted absence of letters, this mere shape is your own sign, yourself. After this dream the self-doubts ahead may prove to be unbearable.

Killing Time at the Launderette

A warning dream. A project, proposal or other initiative will be rejected not because the idea is bad but because your description of it is poor.

If other customers at the launderette try to talk to you the meaning of the dream is reversed.

Kitchen Units

A dream of order, tending to restriction.

If the units don't fit together properly there will be a rebellion.

If the doors and handles aren't matching the rebellion will succeed.

A dream of kitchen units in a state of disassembly, lying around the place for months on end still half in the cardboard and bubblewrap packaging and gathering dust is a premonition of marital strife.

To dream that one is installing kitchen units with the help of a stranger foretells of the arrival of children, the loss of something precious, the discovery of an unopened letter.

Knickers Stolen from a Washing Line

Fidelity in friendship.

Kryptonite

To dream of this most dangerous of substances predicts hidden enemies, conflicts and obstacles.

If the kryptonite is intended for harmful use against Superman the dreamer should be on special guard against betrayal or attack by colleagues, workmates and family members.

If the kryptonite dreamed of occurs in nature – deep in the ground or in some crater following a meteorite storm – the dreamer should beware more

128

the dangers caused by his or her own actions,
agendas and itineraries.

Kung Fu Movie in which you can See the Wires
     See **Wire Fu**

L

Lab Rats

To dream of lab rats, pure white and destined for death, is a sign for the dreamer to sit back and take it easy – the future will look after itself.

If the rats are **in a maze** the dream reflects a life soon to be filled with numerous choices. If the maze is **featureless and white** the weeks ahead will see the dreamer facing a glut of petty dilemmas of an uncompelling kind.

If the lab rats are being used in a **drug test** the dream stands for deception, wounding, subterfuge.

If the rats have had **electrodes implanted in their brains** the dream foretells of a period of much needed rest and relaxation.

Most dire of all dreams involving lab rats is that these unfortunate creatures have been **pinned to a slab and dissected**. The dream suggests burglary of your house, loss of personal direction, the robbery of intimate possessions or the loss of credit cards.

Laserquest

You will become a target.

Laundering Money

Common are the Modern Dreams which involve the transformation of things illegal into those apparently legal. Laundering money is a sign of a promise that will be broken.

A dream of **turning back the mileage clock on a car** is a dream of nostalgia which must at all cost be resisted: the faster the numbers run backwards on the car clock the stronger the nostalgia which has to be fought.

A dream of **hand-stitching designer labels into cheap counterfeit clothing** predicts happiness caused by love, hard work and good health.

See also **Taxi with a Fixed Meter**

Laughing Gas   False relations, deceit, disorder and/or disharmony.

Lava Lamp   Ebb and flow, change, birth.

If the lava lamp is **broken** – the movement of its orange substances slow, indolent or lacklustre – the dream predicts illness, depression or general fatigue.

Lawn Sprinkler   Tears and suffering.

If **the dreamer is leaping through the spiralling arcs of water droplets** thrown out by the sprinkler the meaning of the dream is reversed.

Lawrence, Stephen

A dream of the murdered black teenager is a symbol of family, supportive and strong.

Leaking Waterbed

Ill health, long and painful, will come directly to the dreamer of this dream.

Learning a Choreography Based on the Movements and Actions Described in a Life-Saving Manual

A dream of repetition and frustration leading to happiness.

If the dreamer **continues** in the task there will be success, if she or he **falters** there will be failure.

Led Zeppelin Reunion

Led Zeppelin are a symbol of excess and decadence from the 1970s; to dream of them means that you will be purchasing some new denim clothes in the near future.

See also **Beatles Reform** *and* **Bangles Reform**

Legs Tangled in a Multi-Gym

A dream that one becomes entangled in a complex piece of fitness equipment is an omen of family strife.

See also **Excercycle**

Leisure Centre   Such large off-white structures of concrete, tile, painted girder and glass stud the landscape of many

Modern Dreams, auguring ill for those intent on love, pleasure or spontaneity.

To dream of a leisure centre which has **vending machines in its foyer** predicts financial troubles, whilst a dream that one visits a leisure centre to **attend a trampoline class** predicts a turbulent time for the heart.

A dream of **eating leisure centre food** denotes unrequited love.

Lethal Injection A promotion, new responsibilities, happy memories which may, after time, leave a bitter taste.

Letter Bomb To dream of **making** a letter bomb foretells steadiness in love, courage in business, steadfastness in hope.

Liberace Great loneliness and despair will come to he who dreams of the cynical, bejewelled and besequinned singer whose eyes twinkled as much as the diamonds on his ageing fingers.

Lie Detector *See* **Polygraph Test**

Life is Being Performed From a Script
To dream that you can see the script from which your life is being performed is a warning to distrust all those in whom you confide.

Lift That Stinks of Piss
You will regret an action from the past if you enter a lift that stinks of piss in a dream.

If you enter the acrid lift **alone** the consequences of your regret will be visited on you, whilst if you enter the lift **with another** that person will share your misfortune.

See also **Stuck in a Lift Alone**

Light Sabre Virtuosity, success caused by intelligence, illness caused by accident.

Lights are Against You
A dream that you are trying to get somewhere across town and the streets aren't exactly that busy

but the traffic lights are against you at every opportunity is a dream predicting intervention by a parent, guardian or governmental body.

If the lights **appear to change just as you approach them** you will face a month of frustration and missed opportunities.

Likeness on TV   A dream in which you see your likeness appearing and disappearing on a TV is a warning not to stray too far from original well-formulated plans.

If your flickering ghost-self looks ill the dream has a further meaning, signifying an end to a period of lies and self-deception.

Limited Nuclear War in Europe

A complex lie will be maintained as if it were a simple truth.

Lip Gloss   Descent from a high place (literal, emotional and psychological), distorted impressions gained of a friend or relation, holidays in obscure places or long forgotten resorts.

Litter Blown in Circles

To dream of an urban whirlpool in which scraps of polythene, paper, dust and other detritus circle in some doorway or corner, propelled by unexpected winds denotes confusion. If **the dreamer sees paper with his or her own handwriting** caught in such a giddying trap the dream foretells of deception or forgery, or the misuse of the dreamer's name in a social or business affair.

A dream of a **single polythene bag buffeted alone in such an eddy, rising and falling, yet never escaping,** predicts entrapment by marriage, by work tenure or by simple obligation.

Locked in a Toilet Cubicle

For the home-maker happiness, for the adventurer frustration and for the drug addict death.

Lonely People A dream of lonely people glimpsed in city streets, through windows of a terraced house, at the wheels of their cars etc., foresees true happiness.

Long Lecture about Not Running the Car when the Tank is Below Empty or What's the Bloody Point of Having a Mobile if You Never Charge it Up or How to Use the DVD Player or Why Don't You Ever put the Fucking CDs Back in the Boxes or Whatever
If the dream lecture is from a partner (husband/wife/lover) you will be greatly pleasured in a worldly way.

If the lecture is from a parent or friend you will face unexpected responsibilities.

Lookalikes A dream of lookalikes is a dream of being replaced. To the worker it means mechanisation, to the lover the end of an affair.

Looking Down at the Crowd from the Top of a Tall, Tall Building
A close friend is plotting against you. Exercise caution.

Lorry Jacking The dreamer is forced from the cab, or forced to drive off route at gunpoint or forced to the floor with head covered by a blanket. In any event, no matter what detail of the narrative, in this dream the cargo of DVDs or mobile phones or whatever gets stolen, never to be recovered. The dream foretells of success in politics or corporate management.

Lost in the Phone System
Whilst many truly Modern Dreams are renowned for their spectacular visual imagery and vivid colour schemes, we must not neglect those cases which emphasise the auditory aspect. In the dream of being lost in the phone system the dreamer calls reception and asks for a particular extension. Having done so the expectant dreamer hears a series of beeps or clicks on the line, followed by a silence which grows longer and longer and longer. After some time the dreamer is disheartened to find that his or her colleague's phone does not ring, and

135

further dismayed to learn that the hitherto friendly voice of reception has 'gone'. Silence on the phone gives way to a soft rushing sound, a whispering breeze which more poetic writers have called an *echoing in the vaults of never*. The scene dissolves and the dreamer awakes, his or her ears still ringing. This dream symbolises travel. The longer the dreamer waits on the telephone, the longer the journey will be.

There are many variations to the dream of being lost in the phone system. The dreamer may be **asked to 'hold'** and, again, face a near-eternity of nothingness in the limbo of resulting silence and electronic rain. This dream symbolises creative misfortune, the severity of which, once again, is determined by the length of the waiting.

A further variation is the dream of being **trapped in an incomprehensible touch-tone phone menu system**. This dream is a symbol of anxiety about the dreamer's garden, or, in some cases, of anxiety about a car.

See also **Noise that Sounds like Rain on the Telephone Line**

Lost Pin Number The pin number is a lucky sign, an icon of your true self, your secret heart and identity. To lose it is an omen of forthcoming disaster.

See also **Password Glimpsed**

Lost Remote Control

A dream of good intentions thwarted. The remote is hunted for beneath cushions, newspapers, magazines, under the dreamer's fat arse, on top of the TV, by the telephone ... but still it cannot be found. A plan will fail, a journey will be cancelled, a labour of love will have to be abandoned.

If the dreamer **enlists the help of others** in finding the remote, or worse still **makes groundless accusations at them for having lost or mislaid it**, the dream predicts catastrophe.

L.S.D.   To dream of the hallucinogen whose chemical formula is L.S.D. 25 is a dream-reminder to pay greater attention to details. The small print of a contract or legal agreement, the intonation in a voice or the tiny cracks in some physical structure could all prove significant, or even vital, in the days or weeks ahead.

Luggage Cart   Unexpected directions, free and open conversations, the prospect of a business running out of control.

Lusardi, Linda   To dream of the pin-up girl is a certain premonition of success, unless she is **opening a supermarket, car showroom** or **mini-mall**, in which cases the dream foretells of a birth in one's family or neighbourhood.
    See also **Spelling, Tori**

M

Mace　　　　The popular self-defence pepper-spray, carried by
many in handbags, glove-compartments or
coat-pockets, is a symbol of peace and tranquillity
when seen in a dream.

Mail Order Bride　A dream of risk. You will make a wild gamble, take
an unexpected chance, stick your neck out at work
or in your private life.

If **the bride is smiling in the photograph she
sends** you will be unhappy.

If **she is frowning** you will find joy.

If **she wears a short sleeved T-shirt with some
incomprehensible slogan** you will have many
children.

A dream in which **the letters written to you by a
mail order bride turn out to have been penned by
another** (her brother, sister, or English teacher)
predicts a career on the stage, involvement in
amateur dramatics or an invitation to speak at a
christening or funeral.

Mail Order Catalogue

You will lose possessions by flood, negligence or
fire.

If the dream is of **masturbating whilst looking at
the swimwear or underwear sections** of the
catalogue you will lose face by cowardice.

To dream of **masturbating whilst looking at the
home improvement and or gardening sections** of
the glossy and weighty tome foretells of a change of
heart concerning some important project in your
life.

A dream of **masturbating whilst considering the
Customer Order Forms and pricing tables** at the

139

back of the catalogue predicts a career in the stock market or in money management.

Malfunctioning Deep Freeze in which Sodden De-Frosted Foodstuffs Float in a Mire of Tepid, Rancid Water

Food put aside for the future has been wasted and as a consequence the dreamer's own future is uncertain.

If **chicken wings** are floating in the water the meaning of the dream may be reversed.

To dream of **losing a wedding ring or other precious personal object in the water** predicts a time of chance and unforeseen changes.

Malfunctioning Sex Aid

You will be pleasantly cared for, in a worldly way.
See also **Inflatable Sex Doll**

Market Forces For the painter fickleness in love, for the tourist a broken souvenir.

Market Research Well-known are the Modern Dreams in which the dreamer is subjected to endless and unlikely mixes of questions concerning products which have yet to be launched, packaging redesigns, political perceptions and speculative dental hygiene campaigns. These dreams foretell of periods of change in the dreamer's life.

If **flash cards** are used the change will be sudden.

If **products are used as samples** for tasting or examination the changes will be slow.

Marx, Karl The much-maligned and misunderstood theoretical father of communism augurs ill for businessmen and members of the aristocratic élite but well for the peasants, serfs and working classes when he appears in a dream.

McDonalds A dream of McDonalds is a premonition of riches to come.

If there is some **special promotional Happy Meal tie-in with a newly-released movie** the riches will come to a close relative.

If there is **a tokenistic attempt to represent world cuisine** (Burrito-Pieces, Le Garlic Burger) the news of riches will come whilst the dreamer is far away from home.

A dream in which **the only free table at a McDonalds is piled high with other people's refuse** predicts a period of unhappiness or grief.

A dream of a McDonald's **gripped in the chaotic vice of a children's party** foretells of a chance meeting which will change your life.

Measuring Skid Marks on the Motorway

The meaning lies in the method used for measuring.

To use a **tape measure** predicts a career in the sciences; to use **string** portends a life spent in struggles; whilst to use one's **hands**, placing them down one after the other, leapfrogging the palms slowly and carefully over the dirty glistening ground, predicts a safe passage through a difficult time.

Mechanical Dogs The dream of mechanical dogs is a dream of friendship and loyalty.

If the dogs are **defective** the friendship will not be true.

Meet-the-People Tour/Pressing Palms

To dream that one is part of a meet-the-people tour pressing proletarian palms in the streets of some godforsaken town or in the food court of some over-lit shopping mall portends a month of isolation.

If one is **greeted with great cheer and good humour** the isolation will be pleasantly endured.

If one is **jeered or pelted with eggs, flans, flour or water bombs** the isolation will be troubled, unhappy, demoralising.

Methadone Clinic Icy weather, storms in the night, silence on a birthday.

141

Michael Jackson Morphing Into a Grizzly Bear
Danger from someone you trust.

Mickey Mouse   The black mouse is a symbol of harmless fun.

Mickey and Minnie together predict an unexpected pleasure.

See also **Cartoons** *and* **Finger in the End of a Shotgun**

Microsoft Company Picnic
To dream of this joyous annual institution is to foresee a romantic encounter.

If **one gets drunk at the picnic** the romance may be short.

If **one retires to the Microsoft Campus to play networked Doom until sober enough to drive home** the romance may last forever.

The copious memorabilia associated with the biggest picnic on earth is also of some, if lesser, significance. A **Microsoft Company Picnic Towel or T-shirt** stands for romantic holidays ahead. A **Microsoft Company Picnic Mug, Baseball Cap or other item** denotes a problem involving women, wine or song.

See also **Gates, Bill**

Mile-High Club   The dream depends for its meaning on the identity of one's partner.

If **one has sex with a fellow passenger lying across the seats and covered by blankets in the semi-darkness as the plane hits cruising altitude** the dream predicts a happy future.

If **one joins the infamous Mile-High Club by having intercourse with one of the cabin staff** the happiness will be but short-lived.

If **one's partner in love-making is the pilot or co-pilot** a marriage is predicted.

To dream of **sex in the toilet** of an aeroplane predicts loneliness.

Militiamen Have Come to your House
　　　　　　　You will be the chief beneficiary in an unexpected
　　　　　　　will.

Millennial Tension
　　　　　　　Someone close to you will exaggerate the scale of a
　　　　　　　problem in order to gain your attention.

Mini-Mall　　　You will be pleased with children, satisfied with a
　　　　　　　day's work, contented by good food.

Minor Celebrity　In the curious counter-logic of dreams minor
　　　　　　　celebrities are often more potent symbols than their
　　　　　　　more successful rivals and role models.
　　　　　　　　　Minor celebrities from the fields of **sports, soap
　　　　　　　opera, news presentation** and **pop** all bode ill for
　　　　　　　you yourself, whilst those drawn from **film,
　　　　　　　gameshows, fashion** and **'the social scene'** all bode
　　　　　　　ill for your associates or friends.
　　　　　　　　　A dream of a minor celebrity who is **sleeping**
　　　　　　　foretells of accidents involving cars, planes and
　　　　　　　garden tools.
　　　　　　　　　With their toupées and hair dye, dandruff,
　　　　　　　dentures, chin tucks and ostentatious designer gear,
　　　　　　　ageing minor celebrities are especially potent as
　　　　　　　dream symbols, foretelling as they do that a future
　　　　　　　of penury and heartache is probable.
　　　　　　　　　If a minor celebrity **comes on to you** in a dream
　　　　　　　your recent plans will have to be changed.
　　　　　　　　　To dream that you are **mistaken for a minor
　　　　　　　celebrity** predicts that the misconduct of friends
　　　　　　　will oppress you with its consequences.
　　　　　　　　　If you are **mistakenly asked to sign autographs**
　　　　　　　you will succumb to the temptations of vanity.

Mirror Ball　　A mirror ball in a dream is a symbol of absolute
　　　　　　　happiness, perfection and contentment.
　　　　　　　　　Seen **on its own in a darkened empty room** it
　　　　　　　tells of peace and happiness for the soul.
　　　　　　　　　Seen **lighting a room in your house, at your
　　　　　　　workplace, or a in favourite place that you share
　　　　　　　with a friend or a lover** the mirror ball signals

143

happiness in that particular area or for those
particular people.

A **broken** mirror ball is an omen of heartbreak.

A mirror ball **discarded** – amongst rubbish in an
alley or skip – is a warning of a happiness that is
taken for granted.

See also **Discothèque** *and* **Hall of Mirrors**

Mistaken for a Paedophile

A dream of acceptance. A move to a new
neighbourhood will bring you many friends, a new
job will find you popular and happy, a new hobby
will bring a circle of love, support and enthusiasm.

Mixing Desk   Truth rewritten by those with an interest.

Mobile Phone set to an Embarrassing Ring

If the tune is '**La Cuccaracha**' the dreamer will face
a period of needless struggle in his or her life,
whilst if the tune is from **Vivaldi's 'Four Seasons'**
the dreamer should expect a journey into the
countryside.

If the tune is **the theme from '2001: a Space
Odyssey'** the dreamer will encounter an intrigue or
mystery.

If the **phone rings to any other tune** the dreamer
must expect hardship for a period of one year and
one day.

If **everyone in the pub stares when the phone
rings** the meaning of the dream is negated and the
period of one year and one day will pass without
struggle.

See also **Holding a Lighter or Mobile Phone
Aloft at a Rock Concert**

Modem   If **the strange moaning and skwaking sounds of
data transfer are audible** as the modem operates
you will lose your voice.

If **the sounds are inaudible** a colleague will lose
confidence.

Modern Fear   Writ large in the genre of Modern Fear is the dream that **diverse objects in your house have been replaced by identical replicas.** The paranoid, unproveable sensation of this dream is uniquely unsettling, confirming its reputation as a king pin of Modern Dreams. The dream portends loss in elections, scandal in government and victory in sport. To those involved in trade or commerce it foretells of certain bankruptcy and ruination.

There are many Modern Fear Dreams focus on **sound.** In such dreams the prevalent low hums, electrical buzzes, mechanical throbs, menacing clicks, and diverse indefinable ambiences of tension produced in abundance in the industrial and post-industrial world are amplified, reified and turned to powerful use in the cinema of sleep. Common is the dream of **a low hum whose source cannot be traced,** which stands for fortune in marriage, justice in law and laughter in the workplace. Also common is the dream of **tape hiss** or that of **a deep mechanical throb, which shakes the floor and slowly rattles the bones.** The former signifies a misunderstanding in words, whilst the latter predicts a difficult transaction, a letter delivered to the wrong address or a phone call from a stranger.

Less common is the dream of **diverse electrical buzzes,** the sound of which are often accompanied by showers of harmless sparks. If the sparks are **orange** they stand for success. If the sparks are **red** the dreamer will suffer disappointment. Where the sparks are **blue** the dreamer will face difficult decisions alone.

See also **Bad Thing Somewhere in the House**

Mod Revival   Peace and tranquillity.

Money Stolen or Eaten by a Vending Machine
Heatwaves in the city, deception in the darkness, lost direction in a park.

See also Visa Card will not Swipe, Currency Changes *and* Chocolate Money

Monologue to Camera

The dream is a promise of fame to come. It is also a warning of great loneliness.

Monopoly

To dream of the board game Monopoly is a bad omen, especially if the game is played by the whole family at Christmas time and people get drunk and the contest and excitement of the game leads to a bitter dispute about some terrible things in the past that were probably better forgotten or not mentioned anymore.

If you have bought all of the yellow ones and all of the red ones and two of the green ones and you have hotels on the purple ones but then your brother gets a hotel on Mayfair and you land on it and go bankrupt you should sit back and find time to reconsider any recent decisions which have important consequences.

To dream of a Get-Out-of-Jail-Free Card predicts trouble with money.

Moon Bisected by a Tiny Slither of Cloud

Separation of married partners, strife between brothers, war between countries, injuries to the eyes.

Moon Landing

To dream of landing on the moon augurs madness, in the dreamer or some close associate.

If the dream is in black and white, with the jittering texture and distorted audio of an early TV broadcast from space, the madness may be incurable, long-lasting.

If the dream involves a carefully-rehearsed piece of spontaneous japery (playing golf, waltzing, being woken by the taped chimes of Big Ben, fireworks etc.) the madness will be short and curable.

To photograph one's footsteps on the moon in a dream signifies a need to look closely at the evidence of recent events and draw difficult conclusions.

Moon Reflected in a Lake of Spilled Oil
Duplicity, double-dealing, betrayal.

Moore, Julianne Happiness, true, without blemish or respite.

Morning-After Pill The dream predicts unhappiness.

Mosh Pit The dream predicts a struggle for love.
See also **Stage Diving**

Movie To dream that you are in a movie has no meaning unless the **precise title** of the film can be recalled. Since each film ever made has its own separate meaning, a full interpretation is, unfortunately, beyond the scope of the current volume and the user must await patiently the efforts of other distinguished scholars in the field of Modern Dreams.

As a crude rule-of-thumb **black and white movies** signify more optimistic possibilities, whilst **colour movies** are more bleak in the prospects they suggest. To dream of a **silent movie**, always, and without question, means the end of an affair.

A movie with **Dolby Surround Sound** is a dream of a touch from a friend or a lover which now seems distant or cold.

MTV You will be happy, friends will be honest and true.

Mug with a Picture on It
If the picture is of a **missing child** the dream portends a rebirth of wonder.

If the picture shows a **missing item of clothing** the dream augurs a disappointment.

Muggings Set against the wall of a piss-stinking alley, a dream of a mugging augurs well for morale. The dreamer will be buoyed up, finding fresh enthusiasm, which will make difficult or stalled projects (from DIY to thermodynamics) seem newly easy and achievable. The more muggers there are the better the omen for the dreamer's morale.

If the mugging is **excessively violent** the dream augurs well for those in politics, insurance or gathering news.

If the muggers are **blind,** or **carry long thin knives** there will be good news for the dreamer's family or neighbourhood.

Multiplex Cinema

The meaning of the dream lies in the number of screens at the multiplex.

Five screens foretells successful partnerships, **ten screens** an abundant family, **eleven screens** ill health caused by negligence, **twelve screens** an unwanted complication in the completion of a job and **twenty screens** achievements which will only be rewarded or enjoyed years after completion.

Multi-Storey Car Park

To dream of the long spiralling exit route from a multi-storey car park is a premonition of a love affair which will end badly, the length of the route through concrete corridors and beneath fluorescent lights determining the length of the affair.

If the dreamer is a pregnant woman or a father-to-be the dream betokens a difficult labour.

To dream involves **living secretly in a car in a multi-storey car park, sleeping hidden by a blanket and some boxes on the back seat with the doors locked,** it is a premonition of wealth and happiness.

See also **Pay & Display**

Murdered with a Golf Club

If the Golf Club is an **Iron** you will find work in industry.

If it is a **Wood** you will find work in Agriculture.

Musical Plastic Christmas Tree in the Deserted Fluorescent-Lit Foyer of the Northern General Hospital Cardiac Wing, December 19th 1999, the Cheap Chip in its Red Plastic Base-Bucket Stuck on the same Fragment of a Tune and Heading for a Meltdown

Things will probably get a lot worse before they are ever going to get better.

Muzak Suddenly Stops
>   You are being warned against intervening in the
>   private affairs of others.

N

Nail Bomb   If the nail bomb **explodes** the dream foretells that
solutions to a problem will be found.

If the nail bomb **lies unexploded in a polythene
bag, sports holdall or the floor of a car** the dream
foretells of a period of desperate and tense
anticipation. A deal will remain forever unclinched,
a letter forever unanswered, a phone call much
wished-for will not come.

Naked on a Chat Show

A warning concerning hygiene or an indiscretion by
a friend.

Naked on a Game Show

A general prediction of contentment.

If the dreamer has **goosebumps** or is **shivering**,
pressing close to the illuminated perspex panels
and flashing lights of the studio/podium/scoreboard
design in order to keep warm, the dream is a
warning about friendship misplaced.

Negative Objects, Places and People

A common sight in Modern Dreams are those
mysterious objects which might best be identified as
'X but not X' or places most often described as 'Y
but not Y'. The dreamer might recall 'a car that is
not really a car' or a drive in a city which is 'San
Francisco only not really San Francisco'; others
speak of being threatened with 'a gun that is not
really a gun', or of buying 'a silver metallic toaster
that is not really a toaster'. Founded on the
profound indeterminacy of the Modern world,
such dreams reflect a significant unease in the
dreamer about the circumstances of his or her life

and the possibilities for true happiness or understanding. Where negative objects and places converge in the same dream, it augurs ill for the dreamer, family and friends.

Related are the Modern Dreams which feature what scholars of the subject have now termed *negative persons*. In such dreams the dreamer may see 'Aunt Rose, only it's not Aunt Rose' or 'Ralph Nader, only not really Ralph Nader': figures whose ambiguity is total since all that is known about them is who they are *not*. Such dreams stand for difficult times ahead, especially in the field of relationships and the family.

If *negative persons* play a large or **central role** in a dream (i.e. the dream involves being married to Andrew Lloyd Webber only it is not really Andrew Lloyd Webber) the dreamer can expect it to be followed by a death in the family or that of a close friend or work associate.

If the dream involves *negative persons* in minor or **incidental roles** (a desk clerk who is Harvey Keitel but not really Harvey Keitel, or a petrol pump attendant who is the dreamer's father but not really the dreamer's father) the dream predicts a birth.

See also **Joined Places, Rooms, Objects and People** *and* **Unknown Electrical Goods**

Neoliberalism	The dream denotes an accident in which some person or persons will be very badly injured.
Nerds	Nerds, especially computer nerds, are good omens and must not be confused with **Geeks**, whose presence in a dream always augurs ill. (Readers seeking an exact differentiation between the two are advised to look beyond the confines of this specialist volume: however it may help to exemplify that, as a rule of thumb, *geeks* have both more spots and more money than *nerds*). Computer nerds in a **location well-known to them** (in an office, Starbucks, or shopping mall)

bode well for one's business or leisure plans, whilst nerds 'out of water' (at the opera, at a dinner party or swimming pool) bode well for one's sex life and romantic interests.

A dream in which two nerds are **making passionate love** is a bad omen.

Nerve Gas

To dream of a nerve gas attack signifies an argument at work, or a dispute about prices.

To dream of a **city after a nerve gas attack** – with bodies strewn in the streets, in the houses and the shopping malls – is a dream of relaxation and calm, contentment, peace.

New Drink

Common are the Modern Dreams of new mixer-style drinks, either actual or imaginary. Perhaps most surprising to some is that the commonest dreams are those involving drinks with brand names which do not exist. Which widow has not dreamed of *Oblivion*, with its ice-white label and bewildering faux-deco art-work? Which new father has not dreamed of *Irrelevance*? Which worker in an abattoir has not dreamed of *Vortices*? In each case the meaning of the dream lies in whether the drinks are consumed or not.

If a bottle of *Oblivion* or some other imagined drink **stands untouched** the dream predicts a future of solitude, problems with money and filial ingratitude.

If the bottles are **empty, drained to the last drop,** the dream predicts love, a swift end to conflicts and a long life in good health.

Night Cleaners

A dream of night cleaners as they sweep slowly through an office block or station terminus signifies change by tiny increments.

If the cleaners work **alone** the dream foretells of a time of privacy and quiet strength.

If the cleaners **speak no English** – communicating in Turkish, in Somali, in Urdu and Hindi or by pointing and smiling and gesturing – the dream

153

foretells of a difficult marriage, partnership or collaboration.

A dream of night cleaners **asleep** – slumped at the desks of their masters, curled in stationary cupboards, crashed out in empty railway carriages – is a dream predicting politics gone sour, diplomacy at a crossroads with failure in both directions.

Nightschool   A dream of attending nightschool, with its bleach-smelling corridors, its shabby classrooms and weary bespectacled teachers, foretells of struggles in youth, unhappiness in old age.

If the dreamer is **studying maths** the dream stands for lost time which can never be made up.

To dream of being **unable to find the classroom** predicts a life of travel, a night of wandering, a future of displacement.

Nightvision   To dream your life in the grey-green colour and texture of Nightvision predicts a windfall of money.

If there are **naked people visible moving about in the dark** you will lose the money very quickly.

Nikkei   The movements of the Japanese Market Index are subtle and unpredictable. To dream of it is a call for caution and for careful planning.
See also **F.T.S.E., Hang Seng** *and* **Dow Jones**

Nixon, Richard   Shame, reluctance, bad luck.

Noise that Sounds Like Rain on the Telephone Line
You will be deceived.
See also **Lost in the Telephone System**

Norton 950   A dream of the classic motorbike predicts a time of freedom from all moral or ethical constraints.

Nose Job   Dishonesty, unscrupulous friends, public humiliation and shame.

NutraSweet   A dream of the tiny white substitute-sweeteners is a dream of true friendship.

O

Objects from the TV Keep Appearing in your House
The dream that a ball is kicked out of play on the TV but it ends up in your house signifies a change in your luck, the change being for the better.

A gun fired on the television with the bullet ending up in your house is a much less favourable dream.

Such dreams are examples of boundary-crossing and may be likened to those dreams where you enter an unfamiliar area of a city or town. To dream that **you board the wrong train and end up in the suburbs** or that **an illegal taxi takes you, unbidden, to a rave near the motorway** signifies a shrinking of your physical and social world, as marriage or work commitments tie you to routine.

Obsession by Calvin Klein
The relationship you are in will be short, if passionate, and will linger in the mind.
See also **Eternity by Calvin Klein**

Obsolete Formats   To dream of obsolete formats, from 8-track cartridge through Laser Disc, Betamax and Hi8 to Super 8, suggests that you need to change your thinking, lest old habits and prejudices do you harm.

Office Flirtation   Success in economics.

Office Furniture   Conformity, pedantry, order.
A well-known Modern Dream is of office furniture **washed away by the sea**. The dream speaks of a conflict between the rational part of the dreamer's mind and the irrational, emotional part. If the office furniture is **borne far away over the**

155

horizon the emotional part will win; if the office furniture stays trapped forever in a circular swell, going backwards and forwards in the region of the shore, the rational mind will win.

A dream of office furniture marked in some places with semen stains is a dream of love that will not last, whilst a dream of attempting to assemble office furniture whilst following instructions from a photocopied sheet is a sign that the dreamer's arguments or position on some significant issue are weak and undeveloped.

Office Party   A life of no surprises.

If there is someone having sex in the photocopying room the meaning of the dream is reversed.

Offshore Banking   Frail memory, sturdy ambitions.

Offside Trap   Problems of love and family politics.

If the dreamer has a goal denied there will be an argument in the bedroom.

Oil on the Surface of a Puddle
Unhappiness hidden beneath the smile of a friend.

Old People's Home
The meaning of the dream is in the smell.

If it is of stale shit and urine you will be rich.

If the smell is of disinfectant, bleach or medicinal alcohol you will prosper in a game of chance.

If the smell is of old clothes and mothballs you will suffer setbacks in business and home repairs.

A dream of an old people's home at night, with all the old people sleeping, is a dream of hope lost to realism, fear caused by memory and ghosts.

'On Air' Sign   You will have to make a calculated risk.
If the sign is on you will succeed.
If it is off you will fail.

On Hold   *See* **Lost in the Phone System**

One Way System   A dream which foretells of a delay in achieving some goal or aspiration.

OPEC   Family troubles, lovers' tiffs, a week of attempted manipulation by neighbours, strangers and friends.

Open Plan Space   If the space is an **office** it signifies good news from abroad, if the space is **a school classroom** there will be bad news from home.

    If the space, littered with free-standing screens, furniture etc. is **indeterminate in function,** the dream foretells that a dilemma will be faced with a lack of composure.

Opening a Supermarket

    You will succumb to adversity and your plans will come to naught.

Operating the Score Board on a Gameshow

    The dreamer sports the rictus of a smile, a short, flimsy or otherwise inadequate costume and a pair of gold-spangled heels. The dreamer's task most often involves staring gleefully into the middle distance of the camera whilst operating some mechanical device or another to rotate letters and numbers in the scoreboard.

    If **the numbers displayed are large** the dream stands for fertility.

    If **the scoreboard gets stuck** the dream stands for impotence.

    If the dreamer gets his or her **costume entangled in the mechanism and has to be freed by the stage manager or lighting technicians** the dream stands for love in an unexpected quarter.

Ordinary People Next Door are Serial Killers

    It says much about the robust constitution of the Modern Dreamer's psyche that this situation is more common in real life than it is in dreams. To dream that the ordinary couple next door are a well-practised husband-and-wife team of evil serial killers predicts uncertainty to come.

157

Outboard Motor   A new venture will receive unexpected help and support from a friend.

Outing   The outing of a celebrity signifies a surprise party.

Overhead Projector

An accident may involve damage to your eyes.

If the projector is **broken** the accident will be serious.

Oxygen Tent   To dream that one is confined within an oxygen tent predicts freedom from some long-resented responsibility.

If the oxygen tent is **steamed up** the dream foretells of a time of confusion and change.

If the oxygen tent is **surrounded by family and friends** the dream predicts an unexpected journey, change of status or promotion.

Great unhappiness will come to those who dream of **a child** inside an oxygen tent.

P

Package Holiday in a Famine Area
> A crisis of faith, belief or commitment to a cause.

Packed Like Cattle on a Crowded Train
> To dream that you, your family, neighbours and friends are packed like cattle on a crowded train predicts a chance for change, which must be seized at all costs.
>
> *See also* **Shot in a Pit** *and* **Temporary Tattoo**

Packed Lunch
> A dream of a packed lunch, with white bread sandwiches curling moistly in a translucent Tupperware container, bruised fruit and a token chocolate treat, predicts that the dreamer will get into a fight.
>
> If **the sandwiches** in the packed lunch **contain a surprise filling** the dreamer will suffer badly in the conflict.

PacMan
> To dream of PacMan is to dream of unnatural hunger.

Paintball
> You will be a hunter at night and quarry by day.

Painting by Numbers
> A dream of truth, decisions or understanding that comes slowly, piece by piece by piece. The dreamer will need patience and calm to think ahead, and a steady eye and hand. Assuming all of these the future can be bright.
>
> If the dreamed picture is of **a horse in a field** the dream portends capture for the criminal, freedom for the just.
>
> If the picture shows **fornication in a range of lurid pinks and numerically graded fleshtones** the dream predicts silence from an old friend.

Palimony   A dream of love. The higher the palimony amount dreamed of the greater the love will be.

Particle Accelerator

Those who dream of the vast circular track of the particle accelerator at CERN will triumph and prosper in a love that succeeds against the odds.

Party at the Playboy Mansion

If there are **Playmates ©️ swimming in the pool** the dream foretells that you will rise to honour and amass great fortune.

If the pool is **empty or drained**, or if its surface is **patterned with a covering of leaves, litter and abandoned thongs** the dream foretells disaster.

If **Hefner attends the party** you will have merry news of absent friends.

Password Glimpsed

The dream of a password glimpsed is complex and has many variations in which the password is overheard, glimpsed as it is typed, or seen on some scrap of paper left indiscreetly at a desk or by the telephone.

If **the password glimpsed is your own** you will be guilty of a violent outburst, attack or even murder.

A dream that you have glimpsed the password of **a stranger** foretells that you will catch an unexpected illness.

A **password which has been changed** indicates unseasonable weather, whilst to dream that **you have forgotten your own password** is very dangerous indeed, predicting prolonged ill health.

In the worst of such dreams of **forgotten passwords** you type again and again bizarre and near-meaningless combinations of alphanumeric keys, trying upper and lower case, trying the names of friends, lovers, heroes, children and pets in backwards combinations until your eyes are burning from the screen, your fingers cramped from the keyboard and all with no success. Such dreams, like the dream of being **locked out of the**

160

building because your swipe card has buckled can mean only one thing – an early death, and no escape from it.

See also **Lost Pin Number**

Pay & Display Pay & Display parking is a symbol of strength in friends when it appears in a dream.

See also **Multi-Storey Car Park**

Peace-Keeping Force moves into your Pub

The presence of UN/IFOR delegations checking identity papers on entry and exit from the toilets and keeping the rival factions confined to the bar and lounge respectively predicts trouble at a wedding, funeral or football match.

Pedestrians Fall into Step with You

A common Modern Dream which generally stands for the opposite – you will find yourself alone. To the lover it spells desertion, to the academic ridicule, to the yachtsman a serious storm and damage to a compass.

Perfect Lawns A dream of smooth, lush, well-manicured and deep green lawns foretells of health and beauty for a child.

Pet Beauty Parlour Troubled hearts, wandering eyes, a life rocked by mental disturbance.

Phone Call Lasting Five Days

The dream is an eternity of talking and talking, listening and listening. The clock ticks, the sun rises and sets and rises and sets, darkness falls and is banished, falls and is banished again and still the phone call continues.

If the conversation is about **money** the dream signifies the rapid end of innocence or the start of a crisis.

If the conversation dwells on **love, romance** or **intrigue,** the dream signifies great progress at work or in the realm of the dreamer's garden.

If the talk is **nonsense** or merely the **long, long**

161

exchange of near-incomprehensible numbers the dream predicts accidents, emptiness, death.

Phone Stops Ringing as Soon as You Get to It
A dream of a thwarted romance.

Photocopier
A photocopier in a dream augurs its opposite: the machine which produces an endless supply of replica items is a powerful symbol of originality and invention.

A dream of a copier **alone** foretells of a period of creative productivity, whilst a dream of **tending a photocopier as it churns out copy after copy after copy** predicts that you will soothe and support a colleague or a partner through some difficult and protracted process of invention.

A dream of a photocopier **upon which personal or sensitive documents have been left** (intimate photographs, love letters, diaries, tax returns, top secret memoranda, etc.) augurs ill for the dreamer who will suffer from embarrassing revelations.

Photofit
To dream of one's own face as a photofit foretells of a period of self-doubt.

In a similar dream one sees **one's own face on a poster produced by a police artist, features reconstructed crudely in pencil or graphite.** This dream represents misgivings about a recent financial or emotional transaction.

Photographs from Holiday are Overexposed
To dream of returning from SupaSnaps bearing stacks of holiday photographs, all horribly overexposed, is a not a common dream; but it remains an important one. The bleached-out faces, flash-whitened skins and brutal red-eye of your friends and family are a fragment of a holocaust predicted for the future. That the resurgence of some local or military conflict or world war will follow this dream is as certain as that day will follow night.

162

To dream that the holiday snaps which you have collected are **not your own** foretells break in family, unease in relationships and replacement at work.

Piano Thrown from the Window of a High Rise

The piano may be surrounded by curious onlookers as it lies broken on the dirty paving slabs amongst the pigeon shit. In this case the dream betokens an interest in music.

If the piano **has killed or injured someone on landing** the dream betokens the onset of a turf war between rival triad gangs.

Picking Labels off a Beer Bottle

As in the common Modern Dream of **Skinning Beer Mats** the dreamer is being warned against insincerity in associates at work or in the playground.

Picture of a Stranger in Your Wallet

The dream involves searching for a stamp or credit card and the accidental discovery of a portrait or passport photograph, depicting a stranger. The stranger in this dream stands not for another but for some neglected aspect of the dreamer's own self.

If the stranger pictured is **handsome** or **beautiful** the dreamer has neglected his or her looks.

If the person is **smiling** the dreamer has neglected his or her happiness.

If the person is **weeping** the dreamer has been moving fast, covering tracks, acting in denial of his or her true feelings.

If the photograph of a stranger found in a wallet has been **scratched through with biro, eyes erased, or face disfigured with the point of a compass** the dreamer will enjoy an old age, kind children and blissful contentment.

163

Pierced Navel
A dream of a pierced navel warns of bad news for one's father and mother.

If the piercing is steel the news will involve an accident.

If it is a diamond the news will mean the death of love.

Pigeon Loose in the Carriage of an Underground Train
To see a pigeon or other bird loose in the corridors of an underground or subway system is a bad omen. If the bird panics and flies against the glass the dream denotes trouble caused when the dreamer falls into bad companionship. If the bird boards a train the meaning of the dream is reversed. In the worst of these dreams, all premonitions of personal downfall, it is not a bird but some other animal (reptile, monkey, tropical insect) that wanders loose in the subway system.

Pirate Radio
You must listen to your hidden, secret or forgotten desires.

Pissing in a Carpark
The theme of pissing in public places runs through many Modern Dreams.

For a man, pissing in a car park denotes unswerving loyalty in a time of crisis. To piss through a letter box denotes the arrival of unexpected news or the arrival of an unwelcome old friend. To piss in a litter bin denotes a big drop in the dreamer's self-esteem.

For a woman the meaning of such dreams is more obscure, bound up as it is with the difficulty of urinating in many places. For a woman to piss in a car park predicts wealth and good health, to piss through a letterbox predicts a career as a contortionist, and to piss in a litter bin predicts a short stay in hospital.

164

Pixilation	To dream that one's skin is pixilated, a surface of multi-shaded polygons in whites, creams, pinks and browns, foretells of a future in chemistry. *See also* **Texture Dreams** *and* **Formica**
Plastic Cutlery	You will be rich.
Plastic Flowers	True love, deep and understanding will come to he or she who dreams of plastic flowers.
Plastic Litter Bin	*See* **Remains of a Plastic Litter Bin Still Hanging from a Lamp Post in the form of Twisted Black Dripping Shape, Completely Melted, Because Someone has Set Fire to It**
Plastic Surgery	A dream of plastic surgery is generally a good sign for business and other prospects unless the surgery is **indistinct or strange,** in which case the dream foretells of bankruptcy or mental health problems. *See also* **Breast Implants**
Platform Shoes	Profit from the ignorance of others. If the shoes are **multi-coloured** – with flashes of green, red and yellow in them – the gains predicted will be very substantial. To dream of being **unable to walk because you are wearing a pair of ridiculous very high platform shoes** foretells of a boost to your confidence. *See also* **Holder, Noddy**
Platinum Card	You will be fooled but your heart will be made stronger as a consequence.
Playing Dead	To dream of playing dead **using tomato ketchup, splattered all over your shirt, daubed on your lips, smeared across your cheek** predicts a month of intense and extreme sexual pleasure. To dream of playing dead **wearing a series of small explosive charges taped with Elastoplast under your** shirt to simulate gunshots when they are triggered by radio remote control foretells of a court action, a criminal prosecution, or a private investigation. To dream of playing dead **by covering your**

165

naked body in unscented talcum powder, lying perfectly still on the floor and staring at yourself in the mirror and getting more and more scared predicts liquidation for a business, incarceration for a thief and wedlock for a womaniser.

Playing Hide and Seek in an Old Deep Freeze

You are scared. To hide in a deep freeze is a premonition of defeat, discomposure, not coping.

To close your eyes whilst hiding in a deep freeze is a wish for time to stop.

Playing Provos vs RUC in the Playground

In the dream there are two teams: one designated Provos and the other designated RUC. Each team selects an area for 'houses' or 'barracks', somewhere between the school gates and the main building. The Provos team plant 'car bombs' and select locations for 'snipers' and 'mortar attacks' while the RUC team set up roadblocks, interrogation cells and an H-block. Play commences as each team sings patriotic songs, the bombs explode, searches are carried out, prisoners taken and casualties calculated by each side. The dream always ends the same way – not with victory for either side but with a complicated and bitter dispute about the rules, objects and proper procedures of play. Despite its content the dream is essentially one of love for systems. It bodes well and predicts work aplenty for bureaucrats, members of boards of trade, legal clerks and football officials.

Playing Stadiums

The dreamer feels uneasy. Every note, every gesture must be exaggerated, every line of supposedly impromptu patter must be endlessly rehearsed. The dream indicates dissatisfaction.

If the dreamer has to wear clothes with Velcro fastenings in order to guarantee quick changes offstage between numbers the dissatisfaction is very serious indeed.

PlayStation   Riches from idleness, pain from love.

   The greater visual definition and processor speed of the **PlayStation Two,** combined with its improved ability to render complex three-dimensional graphics in real time, make it a powerful symbol in Modern Dreams, outstripping its predecessor by predicting a glut of wealth gained with no effort and an abyss of suffering from love.

Plexiglass   There is a secret which will not be told.

Plug Board   Families divided, passions drained, connections to strangers.

Podium Dancers   Eyes ecstatic, semi-clad and sheened in sweat, a podium dancer at work foretells of success in an important meeting or personal encounter.

   To dream of podium dancers **off-duty (sleeping-in in their chalet, sitting dazed around a pool mid-afternoon)** portends a marriage. If the dancers **still sport some aspect of their costume (lamé micro-halter top, PVC g-string, fur-trimmed briefs or bikinis etc.)** the marriage will end badly.
   See also **Topless Dancing**

Political Map of the World (outdated)
   Such maps in a dream predict a change in one's living conditions.

   If the colours are **lurid** the change may be violent.

   If the dream involves **navigating** using an outdated political map, it bodes ill for those involved in the sciences or in service industries.

Polygraph Test   The polygraph is a well-known symbol for romance. To take a polygraph test in a dream is to foresee a period of crisis in that field.

Polystyrene Chip Tray Pierced by a Wooden Fork
   True love.

Polystyrene Fruit   Such artificial food is abundant in the fruit bowls of showhomes and kitchen showrooms. Unconvincing in appearance (colours wrong, shapes exaggerated or too simple) and unnerving to handle (too light) the fruit is a symbol of stasis in a relationship, problems of commitment vs freedom and independence.

   If **the fruit (apple, pear, banana) is patterned with the tiny bite-marks of a child** the dream predicts a difficult birth or an unhappy birthday.

Pool Party   Thanks to the efforts of a friend you will make light work of a heavy load.

Pop Tarts   You will get an enormous boost in your career due to the intervention of a powerful third party if you have dreamed of Pop Tarts.

Popping Bubblewrap
   A dream of annoyance and irritation to come.

Porn Channel (Scrambled)
   To dream of a scrambled porn channel suggests a cloudy future in the area of the dreamer's intimate relationships.

Portakabins   A dream of Portakabins denotes that you will cultivate ugly or distasteful friends.

Portaloos   Confinement, ugliness, incomprehension.

Poster of an Anonymous Topless Girl Sitting on a Motorbike
   You will meet a charming new person.
   If the **girl is naked except for a crash helmet** you are being warned of flood, fire or domestic calamity.

Pot Noodles   A dream of Pot Noodles augurs well for the future.

Power Breakfast   Long nights of work, whispered words in the evening, silent, stretched or stressed-out mornings.

Power Cut   Love at first sight.

Prada Shoes   Prada shoes symbolise commitment.

Pre-Nuptial Agreement
>You will be divorced.

Press Briefing from a Military Spokesperson
>A dream of the opposite – truth and honesty.

Printing Press
>The dream of a printing press warns that gossip will unsettle your position or that rumours will compromise your happiness.
>
>If the printing press is **broken or idle** you will be entrusted with a secret.
>
>To dream that you are **typesetting**, compositing letters made of steel in a huge wooden frame, foretells that you will one day make history.

Private Beach
>Impoverishment of spirit, crisis of finances, loneliness by night.

Private Investigator
>A dream of a private investigator is a dream of the heart.
>
>If the dreamer is **collecting clues, conducting tests** or **following a suspect** a new romance is predicted.
>
>If the dreamer is **being harassed by so-called interested parties** – the police, thugs or mob heavies – the romance may be thwarted by existing lovers or an over-protective family.
>
>A dream of a private investigator also draws some part of its meaning from the quirk or the gimmick of the detective involved. An **untidy detective** foretells debts; a **drinking detective** foretells memory loss; whilst **an abusive and rude detective** (swearing at clients, throwing the phone down on the cradle etc.) predicts peace earned by struggles, strength and solitude.
>
>To dream of a private detective **with an anachronistic dress-sense** (dandy, hippy, teddy boy, late 60s suits, punk) warns of stasis and emotional fossilisation.

Private Prison
>Unhappy love, dissatisfying work, marriage for money or social position.

169

Privatisation	A dream of struggles and emotional wars.
	If the privatisation programme masks **cut-backs, sell-offs, redundancies and asset-stripping** the meaning is reversed – a time of easy prosperity and good fortune is predicted.
Product Launch	The revival of old enmities, discovery of new passions.

Product Placement

Some believe that in recent years the reach of advertisers and brand-developers has extended into the netherworld of dreaming and that, with psychics and mentalists in their employ, the chiefs of the logo-centred world can place their trademarks, straplines and products in any mind, in any dreamer's narrative or space.

Whilst many Modern Dreams are indeed crowded with branded products, often out of context, competing with one other for attention at both the centre and the alleged periphery of the action, the author of this book is not persuaded by theories of supernatural conspiracy in advertising. It is his preferred belief that the Modern psyche effects its own games and projects of product placement, with quite different agendas and purposes in mind.

A dream in which **products from Sony, Panasonic, JVC and TDK** are conspicuously placed predicts the acquisition of an unexpected friend.

A dream in which **cars by Saab, Nissan, Toyota or Mercedes** are placed foretells of ease of passage though life's many trials and tribulations.

A dream in which **products or clothes by Cartier, Rolex, Lancôme, Tommy Hilfiger or Diesel** appear with their labels and their logos perpetually on view is a dream of success to come, its arrival slow but not less useful for that.

A dream in which **a conversation is peppered with brand names, some of them utterly unfamiliar,** is a dream of exile, exclusion, death, degradation and distance from one's emotional and physical centre.

Product Recall Lost directions, news of strangers in daylight, news of family by telephone.

Pro-Lifers Beat you in an Abortion Debate
A dream of a crossroads, whether personal or financial.

If there are **pro-life protestors on the courtroom steps dressed as skeletons** you will suffer heavy losses.

Propaganda Leaflets Dropped from Planes
The dream starts with the drone of distant engines against a darkening sky. As the yellow sheets start fluttering down the inhabitants of the city come out of their shelters and from the ruined buildings with bomb holes that make them look like blackened skulls. The leaflets, if read, tell twisted lies of hatred, violence, degradation. A dream of spirits broken, good fortune reversed.

Property Ladder Promotion if ascended, redundancy in descent.

Prozac When Prozac appears in a dream it foretells of happiness, with one single exception, namely the dream in which **you are doping your spouse or children** with the drug **against their will or knowledge**. This dream predicts that your business will suffer or that death and sorrows will soon come close to you.

Pub Hypnotist A dream involving a pub hypnotist depends for its meaning on the reaction of the crowd.

If **the drinkers are amazed or stunned into concentrated silence by the shoddy mesmeric feats** the dream augurs well for those in politics, press, PR and the media.

If **the drinkers remain cool and indifferent** the dream foretells of a change in management, government or family circumstances.

A dream in which one is **hypnotised into**

thinking that one is a chicken (parading the
beer-sodden stage on hands and knees, flapping
one's arms and squawking in distress at the
approach of an imaginary fox to the great
amusement of all present) predicts happiness in the
home.

Punishment Beatings

The diverse methods of beatings and other
punishments carried out most commonly by
paramilitary organisations each have a separate
meaning. As a rule of thumb the more brutal the
punishments the more positive the omen in a
dream.

A **simple beating** is a sign for general good luck
whilst **knee-capping** or **tarring and feathering**
foretell of an excellent change of fortunes.

To dream of **a paramilitary execution** is a sign of
absolute happiness to come.

Push-Up Bra

Help from strangers, new friends and hidden allies.

If the bra leaves **a nasty set of red marks or
imprints on your skin** the dream warns of
emotional traps set in memories.

Pyramid Selling

To dream of Pyramid Selling means that there
will be an additional member to your family very
soon.

Pylons are Surrounding the House

The dreamer senses movement out in the darkness
beyond the house, but cannot see its origin. The
earth shakes with thunderous footsteps, the trees
shake and lose their leaves. The dream ends with
daybreak and the opening of curtains to see that
pylons have surrounded the house, tearing wounds
into the earth where they have dragged their feet
along. The pylons are so thick that they block the
sun from the sky with their great outstretched steel
arms draped with snapped cables, dwarfing the
house and all other aspects of the landscape. The
dream foretells a season of disquietude.

If the pylons have blocked the roads, the driveway or the doors the season will be long.

A closely-related dream is that of Satellite Dishes which move slowly to encrust the outside of a house, the whole surface covered, windows blocked. The dream predicts an accident, blindness or skin complaint.

Q

Quake

To dream of playing the popular first-person shoot-'em-up game Quake predicts a long, perilous and frustrating journey to a land one has not seen before.

To dream of playing Quake **on a network** is a dream predicting love between neighbours, disputes with strangers and unwise arguments in public places.

Quango

Self-preserving, self-serving, nebulous of purpose, amorphous in action, malevolent and shadowy even in the fluorescent-lit corridors of its own basement headquarters, the modern quango is a symbol of threats in the night, impossible obstacles, disappointments in love and money, struggles with the soul.

If the dream involves **working as an employee of the quango or being subcontracted to provide services on its behalf** it predicts a period of stasis, a plateau in the progress of plans, a relationship on hold.

If the dreamer **wears a suit or sits in a cubicle inside a vast office** the stasis will slowly transform into backsliding, love problems and demotion at work.

If the dreamer sees **a diagram of the structure of a quango, its myriad interlocking committees, consultancies and advisors, its double helixes of executives and chief executives, commissions, contractors and sub-contractors** the dream predicts a period of personal confusion and lack of accountability.

Such complex structural diagrams are a common

175

feature of Modern Dreams, the attempt to render an unintelligible reality made concrete in biro, chalk or marker-pen. The meaning of the dream is often linked not so much to the content (a schematic of a website, a flow of income and related purchasing demographics, the structure of a soap opera narrative, etc.) but rather to the state of the diagram itself – if it is **clear and confident, written on whiteboard** or **computerised**, the future has some clarity; if it is **hand-written, scrawled, full of errors, erasures and crossings-out** the future will be bleak.

A **diagram written on Kleenex** signifies amnesia in a dream.

See also **Circuit Diagram**

Quarantine

To dream that you, your family or family pet(s) are kept in quarantine after a foreign trip is a Modern form of the classic Obstacle Dream.

If your confinement is **lengthy** the obstacle will be overcome.

If your confinement is **brief** you will surely be disappointed.

If the dream involves the quarantining of an **entire house, street** or even **district** it predicts some problems in the love life of the dreamer.

Questionnaire

To be asked to complete a questionnaire is a portent of good luck.

If the questionnaire is **largely multiple-choice** you will prosper in battle or in love.

R

Radioactive Gas   If the dream is of a gas that moves as a dirty cloud, discolouring and staining the skies over a city it predicts uncertainty, plans subject to vagaries and months of indecision.

If the gas is invisible, only detected with the clicking of a Geiger counter, the dream is one of a future scarred by mistrust and suspicion.

Radio Phone-In   To dream of a radio phone-in foretells familial strife.

If the callers are abusive the strife may be serious.

If reception for the station is bad the dreamer may face rejection by spouse, siblings or children.

Radio Static   A dream of the squeals, hisses, noises and stutterings of radio static is a dream of contact with the dead through memories or the machinations of a will.

If there are voices in the radio static the dream augurs well for those who are seeking a new lover.

Ralgex   *See* Smell of Ralgex

Ransom Note   To receive a ransom note in a dream signifies promotion at work or success in one's love interests.

If the note is constructed with letters cut or torn from a newspaper the success will be great.

If a finger, lock of hair or ear is included in the parcel then the meaning of the dream is categorically reversed.

To dream that one makes a ransom note augurs well for those in publishing, graphics and design.

To dream that one is forced to read a ransom

note to camera warns of dissatisfactions with one's status in a current relationship.

Rape Alarm The shrill cry of a rape alarm provides the soundtrack for many Modern Dreams. The significance lies in the place the dreamer hears it.

A rape alarm **heard from the bedroom** denotes romance.

A rape alarm **heard from a balcony or stairwell** denotes a journey.

A rape alarm **heard in the middle of an empty car park or building site** signals that the dreamer faces an unexpected danger.

See also **Date Rape**

Rastafarian Strength in numbers.

See also **Yardies** *and* **Geeks**

Rave Intimacy, solitude.

Ray-Bans Ray-Bans are simple and perennially fashionable sunglasses. They indicate confusion in a dream.

Readers' Wives Fat or thin, beaming, grinning, flash-blinded, legs open naked on the rug beside a coal-effect fire and/or spread-eagled on the floral/cubist bedspread, readers' wives are symbols of good luck, good humour and good cheer when they appear in a dream.

If the readers' wives are **suffering from photographic red-eye** the dream predicts hunger: sexual, spiritual and physical.

If any of the readers' wives are **known to the dreamer** (mother, lover, sister, neighbour) the meaning of the dream is reversed.

Reality TV Riches linked to loss and humiliation.

Receiving Broadcasts in your Head
The dream augurs discontent.

Receptionist Receptionists (like switchboard operatives and airline ticketing staff) symbolise progress, possibility and the promise of the future.

178

If the receptionist is **smiling** in the dream it augurs well for personal success.

The dream of a receptionist who is **showing cleavage, chewing a pencil** or **toying with her hair** foretells that a period of abstinence, sexual or otherwise, is in store.

There are common Modern Dreams of a **blind receptionist sitting at a desk and past whom the dreamer feels compelled to sneak, summoning a lift and ascending to the required floor in silence, without signing in or collecting one of those stupid name tags.** To **succeed** in this surreptitious venture predicts an unfavourable change in one's personal affairs. To **fail**, summoned back to the blind woman's desk with a strict command, signing in with shamed and lowered eyes, predicts a substantial change for the better.

A dream in which one **falls in love with a beautiful receptionist** foretells the arrival of a wonderful gift.

Recession Buster Breakfast (Two Adults Eat and a Child Eats Free)
The dream predicts greetings from a long lost friend.

Re-Entry   To dream of a spaceship or satellite re-entering the earth's atmosphere portends marriage.

If the ship or satellite **burns up** on re-entry the marriage will be blessed with many children.

Reflection in a Shop Window
To dream of yourself mirrored in the windows of a department store signifies certain illness or death, either your own or that of some close friend.

A dream of yourself mirrored in the **windows of an office block** foretells of confusion, disorder and conflicts of interest.

Rehearsing a Pitch The dreamer goes over a ludicrous narrative time and time again, trying to make it more exciting and cinematic. The dream stands for lies told and rumours spreading which must be checked.

179

If **props are used in the telling** the dreamer will
end up doing manual labour.

If the narrative pitched is **resolutely uncinematic**
(a confused non-story, some structureless anecdote
of daily life) the dream predicts success against the
odds.

Relationship Counselling
Long journeys by train, car or boat.

Remains of a Plastic Litter Bin Still Hanging from a Lamp post in the Form of a Twisted Black Dripping Shape, Completely Melted Because Someone has Set Fire to It
A good omen of permanent change.

Remoulded Tyres
The past contained in the present. The future
guided by the past.

Removing Pictures, Notes, Lists and Postcards from a Pinboard
The complex collages of snapshots, postcards, lists,
notes, notices, newspaper clippings and other
personal items built up over time on pinboards (or
the sides of fridges) in kitchens, studies and
bedsitter flats are, in dreams, symbols of one's soul.

To dream of **removing pictures and other items**
is an act of psychic violence, which stands for
self-loathing or dissatisfaction with one's current
lot.

To **remove pictures or other items from someone
else's pinboard** is a sure sign of one's critical
feelings for them, at work or in the home.

Related are the dreams in which the **dreamer
rearranges the magnetic poetry stuck to the
refrigerator in someone else's kitchen.** If the new
sentences are **obscene, abusive** or **provocative** the
dream foretells of a lasting solution to a
longstanding problem.

If the new verses are **romantic** or **surreal** the
dream portends stasis.

Rent-a-Desk
Solitude, loss, incarceration, exile.

Rent Boys
Secrets suspected, sexual tension, privacy invaded.

Restricted Access   A dream of seeing the kids on Tuesdays, Thursdays and alternate weekends is a dream of order, regulation and restriction, each in conflict with the heart. At work or at home the dreamer is facing limitations and unbearable stipulations which demand to be broken or changed. But the dream contains a warning as well as call to arms. Just as increased access to the children will cost the divorcee in terms of time, freedom and cash, the dreamer will face sacrifices for rules which are broken, neglected or changed on his or her behalf.

Revisionist Historians

To dream of revisionist historians augurs ill for the family.

If the errant historians **are attending a convention** the dream predicts unexpected news or revelations about blood relations.

Revolving Doors   To dream of revolving doors denotes a difficult journey.

If the dreamer **becomes caught in the doors** the journey will involve the crossing of mountains.

If the doors **jam, leaving the dreamer stranded on the pavement,** or worse yet **trapped inside the glass cylinder of the doors themselves** the dream predicts a period of illness or ill health.

A dream of revolving doors which **function perfectly** indicates a period of pleasant confusion and change.

Road to Basrah   The long and desolate desert road to Basrah, with its sunbleached corpses, burnt-out tanks and abandoned personnel-carriers foretells that a time of boredom and inaction will be brought on by melancholy.

See also **Schwarzkopf, Norman (General)**

Roadies   Whether sullen, beer-gutted, busy or having a laugh, the roadie is always a bad omen in a dream, predicting exhaustion at work, infidelity in love and the tarnishing of dreams or ideas.

181

If the roadie is **wearing an official tour T-shirt** his meaning is reversed.

To dream of a roadie **changing a microphone during a live concert** augurs ill for those involved in commerce, politics or management, whilst a dream of a roadie who is **sleeping, crashed out amongst the debris and detritus of the crew bus** is a dream of deep problems rising rapidly to the surface.

See also **Groupies, Hoodlums** *and* **Hooligans**

Robben Island	The Modern world is increasingly full of significant and terrible architectural structures connected with repression but now in a state of emptiness, touristic renovation or disuse. It is no surprise that these structures, bereft of purpose in daily life, have become powerful symbols for the Modern unconscious.

To dream of Robben Island is to dream of a secret and hidden past.

The dream of **Auschwitz, the Stasi headquarters in Berlin, the camps on the Gulag, Alcatraz** and even **the gutted and abandoned Doncaster Jail** is to dream of one's own lust for power.

Most telling of all is the dream of **sleeping alone in a disused penitentiary.** In this common dream one is both prisoner and guard, captive and keeper. The dream denotes a struggle – to live one's life as one always has done, or to change it.

Robots	*See* **Wife and Children Have Been Replaced by Robots**
Robotic Dancing	The dream concerns control.

If the dancing is **measured and calm** a final round of an ongoing crisis is predicted.

If the dancing is **frenzied**, order will prevail.

Rockumentary	A dream of riches to come. The more off-the-wall and hand-held camerawork there is, the more wealth there will be.

If the rockumentary has a *sotto voce* introduction

182

by some serious music journalist the meaning of
the dream is reversed.

See also **Docusoap**

Rohypnol (Flunitrazepam)

The so-called drug of choice for date-rapists is a
symbol of power in a dream.

Roll Bars   The protective roll bars of a Jeep or motor racing
vehicle portend safety and warmth wrapped tight
in the arms of a parent or lover.

Roll-On Deodorant

A dream of shame. A thing known, found or
owned will have to be hidden. A hidden thing will
be revealed.

Roll-On Roll-Off Ferry

Support from friends, classmates and neighbours in
completing an arduous or especially thankless task.

Roller Shutter   A dream of a metal roller shutter, commonly used
to secure shops at night, means that a big change is
on the cards.

If the roller shutter makes **agonising sounds** the
dreamer will find contentment in the house of a
stranger.

If it **jams or breaks** the contentment will be
short-lived.

Roussos, Demis   You will fall in love with an exotic stranger.

Rubber Bullets   A dream of rubber bullets for a **man** denotes
impotency.

A dream of rubber bullets for a **woman** denotes
hidden lesbian tendencies.

To dream that one is **struck by a rubber bullet
during protests at the WTO** foretells of a windfall.

Rubik's Cube   A dream of frustration.

If the colours **match up** the dream augurs badly
for those in love.

Running Out of Petrol

The meaning of the dream lies largely in the long walk through dusk or darkness to find the nearest petrol station.

If **cars pass you as you walk along the hard shoulder** you will be lonely.

If **no cars pass** you will find an early grave.

If you **meet a stranger on the road** the coming weeks will produce an unexpected opportunity which you should seize at any cost.

Running Up the Down Escalator

The faster the dreamer runs the faster the progress of the escalator in the opposite direction. The dream predicts a crisis or confrontation that is long overdue. Such Modern Dreams of stasis or physical incapacity are common, reflecting restrictions both physical and mental.

See also **Urban Gridlock** *and* **Tied at the Waist with Elasticated Rope**

Rush Hour

To dream that one is stuck in rush hour traffic, forever reversing or trying to change lanes or change routes in order to avoid the most crowded and motionless streets is a dream of a problem which has now reached it peak. In the days which follow the dream there will either be huge change caused by explosive action or else a slow and gradual diffusion of a situation.

Russian Prostitutes

The lobbies of hotels in post-Perestroika Dreamland are often haunted by wraithlike teenage Russian prostitutes, lithe, blank-eyed and dressed in lime-green Lycra.

If the girls **speak English other than sex-words and money-talk** the dream is one of good fortune.

If the girls are **sleeping, drunk, stoned or have passed out on the leather sofas of the Carlton/Ibis foyers or fake marble residents' bars** the dream foretells of a change of heart or change of address.

If a Russian prostitute **cries** the dream is of rain

or of floods. If she **vomits,** flat belly heaving as she
bends over the hotel bedroom sink, the dream is of
storms. The strong connection between these
post-soviet whores as they appear in dreams and
the weather is inexplicable, a secret which remains
unknown to all but sleep's mysterious master.

If a Russian prostitute **snorts cocaine** the dream
is of snow.

If she **bleeds** (from a wound, from her nose, from
her period) the dream predicts a heatwave, and
with it the violence we have so often seen and have
now come to expect.

S

Safebreaking
Sex, especially mutual masturbation, is predicted in a dream of safebreaking.

Saline Drip
Happiness is denoted by a dream of a saline drip. The translucent bag on its wheeled steel frame is most auspicious when **full of life-saving fluid.**

Sanctions
The dream predicts sanctions – it means precisely what it says. The poor will suffer, the rich will not, whilst those intent on trading will find a covert or back-door way to continue. Literal dreams of this kind are a uniquely Modern phenomenon.

Santa's Grotto
To dream of the virtual winter wonderland of a department store or toy shop's Santa's Grotto foretells a disappointment. The more visible the construction of the grotto (from painted plywood, polystyrene, cardboard, Styrofoam etc.) the greater the disappointment will be.

If the grotto has **a winding miniature railway track leading to Santa's lair** you will face struggles in achieving some important ambition or goal.

If the dream involves **only Santa** your hardships will be caused by a single powerful enemy; if the dream features **Santa with a consort of elves** the strife will come from many quarters.

A dream in which **Santa and elves alike are scarcely maintaining character – making bored and cynical wisecracks under their breath, stinking of booze, slipping out to the edge of the UV-lit fake-snow vista for a surreptitious cigarette –** augurs ill for the dreamer involved in subterfuge or deceptions.

Satan's Slaves
See **Hell's Angels**

187

Satellite Hacking   To dream that you are hacking into a satellite's control system, is a reminder to the dreamer of neglected duties.

If the satellite has **crashed** or been **knocked out of orbit** expect a period of plodding and working in an all-too-familiar rut.

Satellite link-up goes down
You will be blinded or your face disfigured.

Scan   A scan which shows a healthy baby foretells trouble caused by pranks or mischief.

If the dream is of a scan that **shows a baby with more than the requisite number of fingers** the dream predicts theft, forgery or trouble with the law.

A dream of a scan which shows **a baby with no heartbeat** foretells that a parcel wished for will never arrive in the post.

Scargill, Arthur   The appearance of Mr Scargill in a dream betokens conflict.

If **his hair looks messy** the conflict will be sustained.

If **his suit is ill-fitting** it may be over by Christmas.

If the ex-leader of the National Union of **Mineworkers fills the air with powerful rhetoric** you will need to take action of a dangerous kind.

School Children in Uniform, Walking in a Crocodile
Such crocodiles of identically dressed schoolchildren, weaving hand in hand, chattering and giggling, their eyes cast largely to the floor roam the locations of many Modern Dreams.

If the children are **in a crowded street**, disrupting the flow of pedestrian traffic the dream stands for stormy weather.

If the children are **alone** – crossing the concourse of an empty railway station or circumnavigating some bold and useless piece of public sculpture – the dream stands for a courtship that will fail.

188

A crocodile of schoolchildren that **moves in absolute silence** foretells sporting mishap or even disaster.

School Photograph

Wealth, success and unhappiness will be the fate of those who dream of a school photograph in **black and white**.

If the photograph is in **colour** the dreamer will have not wealth or success but happiness only.

If the photograph **shows the dreamer alone, seated before a tasteful orange backdrop and posed awkwardly with some toy, jigsaw or ornament** the dream augurs ill, especially for those in the manufacturing trades, retail and event management.

A dream of a school photograph in which **the dreamer appears twice** – once at each end of the long lines of standing, crouching or seated pupils – the dream portends a difficulty in making some essential decision. A full meaning for this particular variation takes its cue from the dreamer's expression. If both the dreamer and his or her mischievous double are **smiling** the dream points to a happy resolution of the dilemma. If **one smiles** and the other **frowns** the dream portends a less-than-perfect outcome, whilst **if both versions of the dreamer have been photographed in the midst of a frown** the dilemma will find no solution at all.

Finally, **the dreamer who is blurred or out-of-focus** in a school photograph will be troubled by a memory or story from the past.

Schwarzkopf, Norman (General)

A dream of this General, distinguished in the US Military Gulf War and other campaigns, is a symbol of strength.

If his uniform is **dishevelled, dirty** or **torn** the meaning of the dream is heightened.

See also **Road to Basrah**

Scientists have taken a Photograph of God

Expectations dissolved, nerves before bedtime, pauses, stuttering then silence in an important meeting.

Scrabble

A dream of the board game Scrabble stands for success in public speaking or in writing.

To dream of **winning** the game predicts the arrival of a letter.

The dream in which one **chokes on Scrabble letters**, struggling to contain or evacuate them from one's mouth, foretells of confusion, bad communication and verbal incoherence.

Scrolling through the Phone Numbers in Someone Else's Mobile

The dream augurs ill for those intent on marriage or corporate mergers, well for those who would travel far and alone.

Seatbelt Tangled

True love, deep and lasting, is foretold by the dream in which one tangles one's seatbelt with that of a fellow passenger.

Most fortuitous of all are those dreams in which the tangle is solved without the utterance of a single word.

Security Guards

With their portakabins, cheap uniforms, bad manners and procedures learned largely by watching cops on TV, security guards (or night watchmen) are a powerful if shabby presence in the structure of many Modern Dreams. With no true meaning of their own in most circumstances security guards have the function simply to cancel (or at other times reverse) the meaning of objects, events, places or situations.

If the dreamer sees a **Swatch**, a **leaking waterbed**, or an **Animal Hospital** in the same dream as a security guard, then the bad news they portend is effectively negated.

Likewise in a positive dream – of a **Fire Extinguisher**, or of **confusing prices at a Motorway Services** – the happy meaning is negated by the simple presence of a night-watchman or security guard.

If a security guard in a dream locks up an object or appears to be guarding it the meaning of the object in question is not simply cancelled but actually reversed. In such *reversal dreams* a positive omen is thus an omen for the worse.

Aside from their function as negators or reversers of meaning there are several situations in which a dream of a security guard or night watchman has meaning of his own. If a security guard has a bunch of keys you will be lucky in love. If he has a topless or swimsuit calendar you will be lucky in lust.

The dream in which a security guard is chatting to an unseen colleague on a walkie-talkie, making crude jokes through the crackles and static, saying 'Fuck it. Over, Fuck It Over, over' etc. warns the dreamer not to focus on distant concerns but on matters much closer to home.

Finally a dream of a security guard/night watchman who is guarding an empty warehouse or building at night, watching the deserted rooms on CCTV, doing rounds on the hour, every hour, to check doors and windows in what better writers have called a 'vast and endless kingdom of nothing' portends well for those who wish to study, travel or make plans for the future.

Seduced by your Babysitter

For a man the dream bodes ill, especially in the areas of commerce and home decoration.

For a woman the dream denotes great pleasure ahead.

Segregated Beach A healthy break with the past, romance between strangers, time spent in much needed private contemplation.

Self-Cleaning Oven

The dream predicts an easy exit from an unloved job or unwanted relationship.

191

Self-Storage
A maze of corridors leading to identical units, numbered, lockable, each piled high with diverse items – machinery, boxes, furniture, archives of paperwork, car parts, fairground rides. The whole place is ill-lit and silent. The dreamer searches, but the object of the search remains forever unclear. The dream is one of ambition, albeit restless and unfocused.

If the dreamer **moves quickly** success is predicted.

If the dreamer **moves slowly** the future ahead is dark.

Sellotape
You have underestimated your connections to your family. Attempts to question or distance yourself from them will not succeed.

Sending Racist Hate-Mail to Yourself
A dream of ambitions thwarted.

Sent Off for Time-Wasting
A shaming dream. Your strategies will be seen for what the are, the stocks of your charm will be emptied.

If the dream involves time-wasting by **endlessly re-positioning the ball for a free kick** or a team which is **changing and then re-changing its mind about who is going to take a throw-in** it foretells of dishonour through uncertainty, problems caused by indecisiveness and procrastination.

Sex Change
For a man the dream suggests a need to better privilege work, for a woman it suggests a need for emotional support.

If the dream of a sex change involves **surgery** it foretells that a week of surprises or travel by plane is in store.

Sex Cinema
To dream of an adults-only cinema is to foresee a meeting between strangers.

If there are **cries or shouts in the darkness of the cinema** you will prosper from the meeting.

If **the projection breaks down** you will lose out.

192

To dream of **cleaning or tidying a sex cinema,
with its detritus of spunky tissues, Coke cans and
discarded syringes**, foretells a future as a housewife
or househusband, confined to chores for long hours
of boredom.

Sex Experiments in Space

To dream that one takes part in sex experiments in
space has three possible meanings:

If the sex experiments are **organised by NASA**
the dream predicts a marriage.

If the experiments are **organised by the Russians**
the dream foretells of an affair.

If the experiments are **informally organised or
simply to satisfy personal curiosity** the dream
foretells of a change in upper management, local
council or national government.

See also **Zero Gravity**

Sex in a Car

To dream of having sex in a car is to foretell of rich
children and plenty of them.

If **the handbrake is sticking into your thigh** you
may have twins.

Sex Therapist

Great success and true love. Honesty in a family,
wealth and health to widows, bachelors and all
those of diverse sexuality.

Sex with an Unnatural Blonde

The dreamer is speechless, paralysed and transfixed
by the contrast between the lover's long peroxide
blonde hair and the dark triangle of her pubic area.
The dream signifies troubles with the past.

Sex with the President

A dream of promotion.

If the president **comes all over your clothing** you
will be famous.

Shakespeare in Modern Dress

Shakespeare is the greatest English language
playwright; his words have given wisdom, humour
and solace through the ages and across every

continent of the world. A dream in which a
Shakespeare play is performed in Modern Dress
foretells of changes in your work conditions or
family situation.

If the scribe's work **has been transposed to the
mobster era of 1920s Chicago** you will be successful.

If the costumes are those of **Nazi Germany** you
will fail in an important enterprise.

A dream of **Shakespeare performed in disco
outfits or bondage punk style** predicts an
unexpected embarrassment.

If a dream features Shakespearean drama
performed by named thespians it augurs well for
lovers, lawyers, writers and all those seeking solace
through drink, drugs or pleasures of the flesh.

Sharing a Taxi with Strangers

To share the intimate space of a taxi with strangers
has a powerful significance in dreams, depending
on the number of strangers involved.

One stranger means happiness, **two** strangers
means decisions have to be made, **three** strangers
means doubts, **four** strangers is a warning, **five**
strangers is a crisis coming to a peaceful end.

Sharing Needles

Someone close to you is a traitor. To the business
man it may be a colleague, to the social security
fraudster it may be a neighbour, to a lover it may
be the object of their love.

Closely related is the dream that the dreamer's
clothes are caught on barbed wire: this dream
foretells of the abandonment of childhood plans
and dreams under the influence of a 'friendly' third
party.

In each of these dreams it is the *point* (of the
barbed wire or needles) which make up a second
part of the message. The sharper the point the
more imminent the danger.

Clothes caught on **razor wire** predict a windfall,
whilst the appearance of razor wire itself predicts
entanglement with a large family.

194

Shell Suit	If the shell suit is **inflammable** there will be dangers ahead.
	If it is **flammable** you will face questions from a colleague or a friend.
	To dream of a shell suit **of an unknown logo or brand** warns against association with people of doubtful reputation.
Shoplifting	If goods are **secreted under** a coat the dream signifies a secret started, kept and revealed in darkness.
	If goods are **hidden in pockets,** or **under other items in a shopping bag** the dream predicts an act of violence.
	If the shoplifting is **a cry for help** – inconsequential items stolen in ostentatious ways – the dream is a sign for a truce between old enemies.
Shopping Mall	You will probably go shopping.
	A dream of **the floorplan of a shopping mall** foretells that you will get lost.

Shopping Trolley Abandoned in the Bed of a Stream

You will be opposed in all your attempts at advancement by scheming and jealous friends.

Shot in a Pit	The dream of being shot as one stands in a makeshift shallow grave is a common one.
	If **one has dug the grave oneself** the dream predicts a strengthening of character.
	If **the grave has been dug by one's neighbours or workmates** it signifies a forthcoming storm, an earthquake or tornado.
	See also **Packed Like Cattle on a Crowded Train**
Sick Building	To dream that **one's workplace** suffers from sick building syndrome predicts good health, long life and wealth.
	If the sick building is **one's own home** the meaning of the dream is reversed.
	To dream that **one is investigating a public building for the causes of its sickness** – testing

195

air-conditioning and heating systems, fluorescent
lights and vibrations from the lift machinery –
augurs ill for those with children or elderly parents.

Signature on your Credit Card has been Completely Erased
You will lose face in front of colleagues following
an embarrassing incident or disclosure.

Silence at the Breakfast Table
You will be happy and contented in the possession
of good and trusted friends.

Silence at the Urinal
You will climb high but fall very hard.

Silence on Television
A dream of disquietude.

If the silence comes when an **interviewee stops
dead while considering a question, eyes working,
mouth slightly agape,** the dream foretells a
confrontation with family or loved ones.

If the silence comes when **the sound breaks
down on the satellite link-up** and the newscaster is
waiting for someone to respond and they do not
the dream is of illness – respiratory, cardiac or
otherwise.

If a silence on television occurs **because a fresh
tape has not been inserted at the broadcasting end,
or because the TV tower has been bombed** the
dream augurs well for all in love, work and play.

Silly String
The amusing aerosol party novelty product in
several colours only means anything in a dream
when the string squirted from inside it connects
two people.

Those **connected** will be married. If **already
married** they will be divorced.

Simpson, Bart
Wisdom gained from age and serious reflection.

Simultaneous Translation at the Breakfast Table
You will be led astray by a foreigner.

196

Singing in the Showers after Football
> Homosexual tendencies.

Singing Telegram   Be on guard against lending money to a friend.

Sink Estates   A dream of sink estates foretells that you will receive many promises but that very few of them will be kept.
> *See also* **Ghettoes**

Sixty-Four-Thousand-Dollar Question
> Distinction in the field of research, academia or intellectual endeavour.

Skateboarding   To dream of skateboarding has no great meaning beyond a minor augury of good luck, but to dream of **the distant sound of skateboarding is a reminder** of some friend you have neglected or forgotten. The more distant the thunder, rattle and scrape of the skateboarding the more important is the reminder.

Modern Dreams are replete with such warnings and reminders engendered in sounds in the distance. The **siren of a cop car in the distance** indicates a lost or forgotten love. The **roar of a far-away crowd watching football or baseball, the sound of their voices carried on the wind above the streets of the city,** warns of a neglected principle or notion. The **sound of a riot, carried up from the valley with breaking glass, the screech of brakes and human voices** stands for impending homesickness in a dream. To dream of **distant ice cream vans, their bells ringing in a merry tune** is a sign of an unhappy summer to come.

Skimming CDs   To dream of skimming CDs on the surface of a great body of water, the disks glittering as they skip across the ripples, is a dream of carefree days ahead.

If the CDs **contain data rather than music,** the dream is of disfigurement and displeasure.

Skin Covered in Hypertext Links

A dream that one's skin is covered in hypertext links is a prediction of a meeting with an old friend.

Skinheads

If the skinheads are **boys** the dream signifies deception, trouble and struggle.

If the skinheads are **girls** it signifies happiness.

To dream of skinheads **kicking down the door of your house** is a very good omen, spelling progress and great success in every aspect of your life.

See also **Gothic Punks**

Skywriting

Messages from friends faraway, aspirations fading.

Slade

See **Holder, Noddy**

Slaughter in a Classroom

To dream that one is hiding beneath a school desk as feckless youths shoot from automatic rifles or machine-pistols, strafing the displays of geography project work and exploding the aquaria, signifies doubts about the past. The dreamer of this dream will be disturbed for many weeks to come, going over events from childhood or more recent times, trying to work out where something went wrong.

If the slaughter **takes place in the playground**, with one's fellows crouching helplessly behind the outdoor play equipment, the dream stands, instead, for fears about the future.

If a **classmate dies in your arms** the dream means that you will be lucky in game of chance or a lottery.

If a **schoolteacher dies in your arms** you will forfeit an inheritance.

To dream that **you are wielding the gun** in this situation is one of the most potent of all Modern Dreams, especially if the action plays out in slow motion. The dream in this form stands for mental breakdown of a slow yet certain kind.

Sleeping Bag

A dream of a sleeping bag foretells a period of well-earned rest and calm.

If the sleeping bag is **zipped up wrongly** you will suffer set backs in important ventures.

A dream of **zipping two sleeping bags together** is a dream of happy families – predicting good cheer and fine conversation in a garden, on a road-trip or at a summer home.

Sleeping in a Doorway Under Cardboard Boxes

A dream which augurs its contrary. Your high ambitions will be satisfied.

See also **Homeless People**

Sleeping Pills Problems solved by spontaneous solutions.

Slow motion A dream in slow motion is essentially a dream of regret. The persons seen in the slow motion dream will suffer ill fortune and possibly death.

To see **children** in slow motion is a certain sign of death.

To see **a lover smile** in slow motion is a sign of love that has now gone or love that will soon have run its course.

To dream of **yourself** in slow motion signifies a distance between present actions and the true path of your heart.

If slow motion **gives way to freeze-frame** the dream signals a need for silence, bed rest and time to reflect.

Water, rain or **flames** in slow motion stand for both change and stasis, each aspect inescapable and profound.

A dream of **death** in slow motion is a dream of its opposite: if **one** person dies in a hail of bullets, passing through the body as it moves like some solo from the ballet, then a child will be born. If **two** die together the birth will be of twins, if **three** die triplets etc. If the dream is of **a massacre** in slow motion there will be births aplenty for you, your family and friends.

A **kiss** in slow motion predicts a sexual encounter that you will have no cause to regret.

Smell of Napalm Victory.

199

Smell of Prawn Crisps

The Modern world has produced smells in abundance, which, though named after aspects of nature itself, bear no relation to it whatever. Sickening, mysterious, strange and delightful, such chemical bouquets have penetrated deep into the netherworld of the Modern Dreamer's psyche.

To dream that **one's fingers** smell of prawn crisps is a dream of regrettable infidelity.

To dream that a smell of prawn crisps **permeates one's house or place of work** augurs ill for the future.

Smell of Ralgex   Persistence of memory, emotional injury.

Smog   A dream that smog covers the city foretells of a period of confusion, especially in family affairs.

If the smog is **especially thick or discoloured** a reconciliation may occur.

If the fog **penetrates interior spaces** (house, workplace, car) the confusion will be significant and the consequences decidedly mixed.

Smoking Outside an Office Block

To dream that one has joined the line of silent smokers in cheap suits outside a tinted glass office building predicts certainty and composure in the face or trials and heartache.

SMS   Silence, the end of a road.

Snapped Credit Card

If the card is **discovered to be broken** you may face bad luck.

If **you** yourself **break the card** in the dream it symbolises a gaining of fiscal control, or an important reorganisation of finances.

To **snap someone else's credit card** in a dream reveals a desire to take control of your life.

A snapped credit card may also foretell that an attack will be made on your garden.

Sniffer Dogs   A Fear Dream, predicting anxieties about secrets and plans for the future.

If the dogs are **straining at their leashes, driven frantically towards you with the apparent scent of some controlled substance** or other the future will surely be bleak.

To dream that you are **petting a sniffer dog in the hope of slipping past it undetected** is a dream of sexual contact, at once pleasurable and frightening.

Soap Actresses   A dream of soap actresses is of only minor significance, predicting an evening of light-hearted fun and inconsequential pleasures.

Soap Opera Family Have the Same Furniture as You
The dream signals future unease.

Social Workers   A dream of social workers predicts a period of personal reflection or reassessment.

If the social workers **are sitting around drinking tea and complaining about the government** you will be surprised by the arrival of a parcel or package.

To dream of social workers **in a fight or an abusive verbal altercation** predicts a change of address.

If social workers **have taken your kids into care** in a dream a sea-change in your fortunes is predicted.

Software   Common are those Modern Dreams in which computer software will not do what you want it to.

If the dream involves **hours of wasted effort** consulting manuals, help pages and truculent telephone support workers, it predicts power struggles at home or at work.

If the software is **Beta Release** the dream predicts a whirlpool of sadness and frustrations.

Solar-Powered Calculator
The dream is a sign of weakness, especially when experienced by students or apprentices, who are being warned that they must study harder in order to pass exams, or gain certificates and qualifications.

If the calculator is **operating of its own accord, doing calculations and sending messages using backwards numbers cleverly combined to spell names and instructions** the dream is a sign of terminal impasse – a situation of strife and conflict will never be resolved.

Somali Boys in Snorkel Parkas

The streets of many Modern Dreams are walked by these lanky, fine boned and displaced figures, their faces shrouded by the extended hoods of their snorkel parkas. Spectres for many redolent of intimidation and strangeness, they have often mistakenly been interpreted as Modern stand-ins for the hooded figure of death (the Grim Reaper), who traditionally carries a scythe. However, their correct meaning is far from this, standing as they do for the prospect of emigration due to love or work.

If the dream involves a **gang** of Somali boys in snorkel parkas it is a sign of impending exile.

Someone is Trying to Bar-Code-Scan Your Eyes

A person who dreams that another is trying to bar-code-scan their eyes is about to receive some unexpected news. The news may be more or less important according to the intensity and colour range of the scanning itself.

Bright red scanning means insignificant news, whilst crucial news is indicated by a scanning light of **softer, more orange** colours.

The identity of the scanner can also change the meaning of the dream. If one's brutal (and strangely motivated) assailant is a **stranger** the news will be a serious surprise; if the scanning is the work of **a colleague** or **an intimate** the news may be banal.

Something Rotten in the Rubbish Strewn on the Floor of the Car

To dream that there is something rotten buried in the rubbish (old newspapers, empty drinks bottles and cartons, discarded plastic sandwich containers,

202

unopened letters, diverse and unidentifiable papers) strewn beneath the seats in the back of the car is a sign of future success which will be preceded by years of hard struggle. The more the car smells the harder the struggle will be.

If the rotten thing is **half a sandwich** the success will be minor and short-lived, if it is **a box of long-defrosted fish fingers** the success will be great and long-lasting.

If the smell rising from the detritus in the back of one's car comes from **a dirty nappy** hidden in the chaos a marriage is predicted.

The sense, in this dream of layer upon layer of slowly-accredited dirt and detritus is a factor common to many Modern Dreams. Who has not dreamed of **the rain sodden and putrefying mess (rotten cardboard, broken glass, polythene, excrement and sundry unidentifiable items) in the corner of an alley,** in which each fragment is evidence for some narrative of suffering and ill-consequence? Or of **the torn paper, fluff, stray coins, dust, grime, sweet wrappers and mystery items found when emptying the bottom of a bag?** These dreams require complex and individual interpretation based on the exact contents of any scene and its grim accumulation of detritus, an analysis which goes quite beyond the scope of this volume. However, the reader would do well to remember that the more unidentifiable, age-worn or broken are the items dreamed in such places the more grave the meaning of the dream.

See also **Fingertip Search**

Soundcheck

To dream that you are present at a soundcheck as an observer foretells that someone close to you will soon find great fame and fortune.

If the music is **Country and Western** you will be invited on an unexpected journey.

If the singer in the soundcheck is **endlessly repeating the words 'One-two … one-two … and er one-two one-two,'** you will have two children.

Source Code A dream in which **you can see the computer source code for everyday objects** is a warning to be careful in your business correspondence.

The more significant dream – that **you can see the source code of a friend or family member** – is a dream of ambiguous intentions. No one should be trusted or taken at face value following this dream.

Space Food To dream of sucking Roast Turkey and Winter Vegetable flavoured slime from a toothpaste-like tube augurs ill for those in business but well for those in services, sports or entertainment.

Space Shuttle If the launch is **delayed** or **cancelled** the dream brings good luck.

If the shuttle **explodes on take-off,** raining debris over many miles, the dream augurs ill.

Spam A dream of junk email or 'spam' predicts a confidence shared with strangers causing trouble in the home.

Speaking Clock The end of a relationship, the start of an adventure, the first day of a new era.

Speak-Your-Weight Machine
Secrets disclosed by friends of ambiguous loyalties, mistakes in a controversial press release, letter or publication.

If the machine **speaks loudly, attracting the attention of others,** doubts and ill feelings harboured for years will finally come to the surface, causing conflict and soul searching.

Speed Trap Danger, perils at work and a need for caution in matters of the heart.

Spellcheck Timidity for the young, and for the old a warning of life lived in an ugly adherence to convention.

Spelling, Tori To dream of the TV actress is a certain premonition of success, unless she is **opening a supermarket, car showroom or mini-mall in which**

cases the dream foretells a birth in one's family or neighbourhood.

See also **Lusardi, Linda**

Spermicide Blocked dialogue, bad atmospheres, poison in a water supply.

Spice Girls The Spice Girls are a symbol of strength in a dream.

If you are 'one of the girls' in the dream you will find happiness.

If the dream involves fucking the Spice Girls you will suffer setbacks at work.

If you are fucking the Spice Girls in some arbitrary order (according to height, alphabetical or reverse alphabetical, hair colour, shoe size etc.) the augury is of money lost in bureaucratic systems and institutional wrangles.

To dream that the Spice Girls have split foretells of ruin for an ill-conceived business plan.

Spiderman To see the Marvel Comic's superhero Spiderman shooting web from his wrists in a dream predicts a sexual problem for a man of premature ejaculation.

If the dreamer is a woman this dream of Spiderman predicts a dissatisfying lesbian experience.

Spilled Ketchup Murder, suicide, death.

Splitting the Atom Divorce.

Sponsorship Deal A warning – not to change your goals but to change the method of approaching them.

Spraying Crops Tears, thick, deep and long-lasting.

Spray Mount The dream of spray mount indicates that a special strand of the dreamer's life will become impossible, untenable or neglected. For the teenager it may mean a broken friendship, for the mother an abandoned career, for the businessman or labourer a hobby which may not be continued.

A dream of a table top covered in a tacky residue formed through the careless use of spray mount foretells conflicts and confrontations at work or in a love affair.

Sprinkler System   A dream of a sprinkler system, whether in a hotel, an office building or an apartment block, foretells conflict and tears.

If the system is **defective** – coming on by accident during the night and drenching everything (computers, paperwork, clothing, furniture) – the dream foretells of grief in an unexpected quarter.

To dream of **installing** a sprinkler system (fixing pipes, connecting water supplies or programming sensors) warns the dreamer of damage done in the present which will surely cause upset in the not-too-distant future.

Squash Court Converted into an Impromptu Torture Chamber

Many are the Modern Dreams in which a range of sporting and leisure facilities are transformed into some inappropriate forum for torture or destruction.

A squash court converted into an impromptu torture chamber foretells of domestic upheaval; a **hotel bathroom used as a temporary holding pen for wanted criminals** foretells of embarrassment in public places; whilst the dream that **one takes refuge in a shopping mall in the aftermath of a nuclear war** foretells of success for a party, picnic or other celebration.

Squeezing through the Railings at a Pop Festival

You will achieve your aims but by unorthodox means.

Stacked in a Holding Pattern Above Heathrow

To dream of being stacked in a holding pattern means that you will need to be patient in the days ahead.

Stadium Disaster   To dream of a disaster in a sports or football stadium portends deceit.

Stadium Rock   *See* **Playing Stadiums**

206

Stage Diving   A dream of stage diving is a dream of losing control.

Caught and borne aloft by the sweating motion of the crowd, the dreamer surrenders to the movements of an undulating mass. To **fall in the** dream predicts bankruptcy, the arrival of debt collectors or a bad year for crops. To **ride on, passed from hand to hand, away from the stage and out to the parking lot beyond** denotes a new direction in the dreamer's life.

See also **Mosh Pit**

Stalin, Joseph   The tyrannical despot of the Soviet Union is an omen of domestic violence.

See also **Graveyard of Torn-Down Statues**

Stalking Someone Whose Name You Do Not Know

The dream has but a minor significance, foretelling as it does a change in policy from some minor official, council or government body.

Standing on a Box so you can Appear to be the Same Height as a Co-Star

A dream of promotion or advancement, at work or in the eyes of a suitor or lover. The bigger the box you have to stand on the greater the advancement.

Stand-Up Comedian

To dream that you are onstage alone, appearing in a sleazy basement night club as a stand-up comedian, foretells that you will prosper in all of your affairs.

If **the band are the only people laughing** the meaning of the dream is reversed.

Stapler   Pleasant losses, unpleasant connections.

Statistics   A dream of **manipulated statistics** is a portent of contentment; the longer the list of massaged figures the greater the happiness will be.

Incomprehensible statistics are a sign of repentance or a change of heart.

Statistics that are wholly and absolutely false have no meaning in a dream unless the dreamer works in politics, journalism or the law: in which case the dream predicts promotion.

Strange Breathing on the Entryphone

Figures from the dreamer's past are often confined to appearing in this way, making incoherent mutterings and the sounds of heavy breathing in the doorway on the street below.

If the dreamer **ignores** these voices a party will be cancelled.

If the dreamer **responds to them** a journey will take place.

See also **Ghost Message on the Answering Machine**

Stealing Paper Clips

Like rocks worn away by water the dream predicts big problems solved slowly, by patience and persistence.

Stealing Time

The dream is of time spent needlessly on daydreaming, or wasted on extended lunchbreaks, and on dawdling in the washroom. The dream foretells of success for the young and premature retirement for the old.

Steam Engine

To dream of such monstrous machinery – tall, dirty, noisy and complex – is to dream of entrapment and lack of control. The bigger the steam engine the greater the forces acting on the dreamer and the fewer the chances of self-determination.

A dream of a **broken** steam engine is a dream of impending change, whilst a dream **that some part of your body or clothing becomes entangled** in a steam engine predicts complicity with those who would harm you or favours received from an enemy.

Sterilisation Programme for People of Mixed Race or 'Gypsy Features'

A shaming dream. The past seeping into the present, certainties threatened and then over-turned.

Sticky-Back Plastic

Disclosures, coverings. Bad news in pleasant surroundings.

Stock Market Crash

A party will go with an unexpected bang.

Stop the City *See* **Battle of Seattle/Prague**

Storyboard Predictable futures, scenarios of entrapment and drudgery. The more **sketchy** the style of illustrations featured in the storyboard the more certain are the perils to come.

Stowaways in the Back of a Freight Lorry

A dream of good luck.

If the stowaways are **dead** the good fortunes will be extended to family and friends.

Strike Breaking To the lover strength, to the traveller speed, to the child sadness born and bred in the company of others.

String Theory Travel plans leading to unhappiness.

Strip Search You will get an unexpected surprise.

Stripogram Jeered at by friends, the dreamer is goaded into removing some last item of the stripogram's clothing, which is then discarded on the beer-sodden floor of the pub. The dream is one of humiliation by unnecessary revelation. Stories will be told, gossip spread, secrets revealed.

If the Stripogram is **old enough to be the dreamer's mother** the dream predicts an embarrassing affair.

If the Stripogram is **a muscle-bound hunk covered in baby oil** the dream predicts a night of loveless passion.

Strobe Lighting A dream of confusion: clarity which fades, or, conversely, uncertainty which diminishes.

Stuck in a Lift Alone

Signifies loneliness.

See also **Lift that Stinks of Piss**

Studio 54   Love found in music, long nights, distant horizons.

Stunt Man   There are many Modern Dreams in which one finds oneself replaced in daily life by a stuntman or body double.

The dream of being **replaced just before a wedding** signifies failure in matters of the heart; whilst the dream in which a stunt man **takes one's place in a coffin** signifies a miraculous escape from a dangerous illness.

To dream that **one's place is taken during an important meeting** (at the bank, with a colleague, for an interview) is to dream of impending demotion or financial ruin.

See also **Wife and Children Replaced by Robots**

Stylophone   A dream of this amusing instrument means you will lose your physical strength due to an accident.

Success Seminar   A troubling dream. Family difficulties, negotiations with memories, strategies arrived at by default.

Sudden Loss of Cabin Pressure

The dream bodes ill for those in politics or business.

Suicide   The Modern world has systematically multiplied both the reasons and possible methods of suicide with a consequent psychic knock-on effect in the world of dreams.

To dream of suicide by **running into the path of a lorry or train** or by **jumping from the roof of a high-rise apartment block** foretells an illness of the body (cancer, leukaemia, A.I.D.S.); to dream of a suicide **using mains electricity** (exposed wires bound to one's own arms, electric fire dropped into a bath) is to dream of rapid and disorientating success.

The dreams of suicide **by microwave, food blender, power drill or jigsaw** are dreams of new employment in the areas of catering and joinery respectively.

To dream of **discovering** a suicide foretells of a birth.

A dream of **a suicide note** is a warning against a gamble which will not pay off. If **the note is written in blood** one would do well to check and double-check plans, to write letters, to make a will.

A dream in which **one sits in a garage in a car with the engine running, the whole place slowly filling up with fumes, slipping towards unconsciousness,** predicts love.

If **the radio is playing as death approaches** the dream predicts a parting.

See also **Talking with a Gun in your Mouth**

Suitcase Full of Cash

To find a suitcase full of cash in a dream denotes different things, depending on the location of the discovery.

If the suitcase is **discovered beneath the bed in a seedy hotel** it predicts a successful party.

If it is found **on a piece of wasteground** it predicts a problem with the supply of utilities to your house.

If, however, a suitcase full of money is found in **the trunk of a rental car** it predicts a future laced with danger and heartache.

To see **money covered in blood** foretells of the loss of a fortune.

See also **Keys to a Locker at the Airport**

Summer of Love (66/86)

A dream of the original Summer of Love (1966, USA) signifies that disturbing and imaginary fears will rack your brain and break your concentration.

A dream of the Second Summer of Love (1986, UK) signifies the same thing only worse.

Summit

A dream of an **international summit, arms talks,** or **extended political negotiations** predicts breakdown in the family.

211

If the talks get close to the deadline and there is **an agreement to stop the clock** so that discussions can continue indefinitely whilst agreement is striven for in a no-time caught between 2pm and 2.01pm, the dream foretells discomfort, stasis or a death by seizure or heart attack.

Sun Bed	Surface changes, touch from lovers, temporary solutions.

Sunblock

A dream of sunblock warns against timidity, whilst **a dream of rubbing sunblock on the shoulders of another** foretells that a time of lonely isolation is on the cards.

If the dream involves **scented sunblock** it foretells of an encounter with a precocious child.

Super-Computer

You will be clever.

Superglue

A dream of superglue predicts unexpected connections as the dreamer's separate worlds (work, friends, family etc.) begin to overlap.

To dream that someone has **superglued the locks to a building** foretells of a period of emotional coldness, whilst a dream in which **the dreamer is glued to another person** predicts an affair.

If the dreamer **becomes superglued to an object** during a dream he or she will be accused of thieving.

Supermodels

The dream is one of fertility. The more supermodels there are in one room the more children you and your partner can expect to have.

Super-Powers

To dream that you have super-powers is to foretell of illness.

Super-sight predicts blindness; **super-hearing** predicts deafness, **super-strength** predicts a muscular wasting disease.

To dream **that a loved one has super-powers** is to dream that they are deceiving you. If you **discover a super-hero costume** (cape, coloured tights, face mask or utility belt) **hidden in the**

laundry of a lover, or at the back of a little-used
cupboard, the deceit is significant and must be
confronted.

Super-Waifs on Heroin

The dream predicts fair dealing in business and on
moral issues.

Suspended Ceiling

A dream of unrealistic ambitions or aspirations
above one's station.

**Suspended Without Pay whilst the Results of an Employment Tribunal
are Obtained**   The dream is one of silence from a friend, a period
of sexual abstinence or a disconnected telephone.

Suzuki 650   Restlessness in front of one's elders, respect for
those who have struggled or made sacrifices.

Swallowed a Free Plastic Gift

Those who dream of swallowing a free plastic gift
from amongst the cornflakes or other breakfast
cereal will tell lies and have them believed.

Swallowing a Condom filled with Cocaine

This classic Modern Dream of smuggling drugs
most often stands for a birth in the family.

If the condom **lies heavy in the stomach** the child
may be deformed.

If the condom **bursts**, the dream stands not for a
birth but for a secret hope, which should not be
given up.

S.W.A.T. Team   Surprises, strangers in bed, enemies on a train, in
trees or on rooftops.

Swimming Naked in Money on TV

Up to the waist in cash, wading through coins and
notes of assorted denominations, the dreamer
swims against the swelling tide.

If there are **other people** in the 'water'
(contestants in whatever crazed show it happens to
be, or girls in bikinis or whatever) the dream stands

213

for a future shared or negotiated, compromised by the plans and desires of others.

If the dreamer swims **alone** the future will be bright, yet determinedly solo.

Swingometer
If the swingometer is **stable** your business plans will go ahead cleanly.

If the swingometer **shifts constantly** the future will be unsteady.

T

Tacometer Discs You will suffer or prosper from something which a stranger has written.

Take-Away Curry If the food is consumed and enjoyed the dream bodes well for those intent on divorce.

If the food is tucked into with vigour but ultimately abandoned in its tin foil containers, the dream augurs well for marriage.

A dream of a discarded take-away, its containers perched and collecting rain atop litter bins or on window ledges or the roofs of parked cars is an omen of defeat in the courtroom, losses in battle, disdain in the bedroom.

Talking to your Parents on the Speakerphone

You have undergone a terrible loss, but wisdom lurks in silent figures to whom attention must be payed.

See also **Conference Call**

Talking with a Gun in your Mouth

If the gun is a **pistol** you will be promoted at work; if it is a **shotgun** you will be fired.

If **you are holding the gun** the dream augurs ill for those in the Civil Service.

See also **Suicide**

Talks about Talks The dream that one's relationship must be solved in a scenario of talks about talks is a rare but important one. In such dreams one finds oneself in a remote hotel or country retreat, speaking to one's spouse or partner only through the mediation of a recognised intermediary. Negotiations are continued day and night, deals are proposed, rejected, modified ... but eventually a deadline is set.

215

If the dream talks **succeed before the deadline and an agreement is reached** the dream signifies failure.

If the dream talks **fail and the deadline is reached with a persistence of dispute and acrimony** the dream augurs success.

Tamagochi has Escaped

To dream that your Tamagochi has escaped means that some fateful occurrence will thwart and cancel the delights that you have been anticipating.

Tampons   The dream predicts a sudden revelation of unexpected intimacies.

Tanning Tunnel   Deep solutions, success from hard work, strength from love.

Tape Drive   Lost memories.

Tape Jammed or Tangled

A dream in which a tape is jammed or tangled denotes a difficulty or confusion with history or evidence. It bodes ill for those about to undertake litigious action, and very ill for those involved in writing biographies. For politicians and the common criminal the jammed or tangled tape dream is a powerful sign of strength and success to come.

See also **Audio Tape Tangled in the Branches of a Tree** *and* **Ghost Message on the Answering Machine**

Taser Gun   The self-defence weapon which shoots electrically charged darts foretells that worldly pleasures, unworldly conversations are on the cards.

Taxi Driving to a Cashpoint

You will be seduced by circular arguments.

Taxi with a Fixed Meter

There is a hidden yet constant problem in the dreamer's everyday life. There will be a chance to discover it but the dreamer must be vigilant.

See also **Laundering Money**

Tear Gas	To dream of tear gas is to dream of a new romance. The more the tear gas stings and burns the eyes the greater the love and the change in one's life.
	If the dream is **accompanied by a soundtrack of rioting** (screams, breaking glass, loud hailers) the romance will end badly.
	If the tear gas works **in silence** the romance will flourish.
	The meaning of a dream of tear gas changes if one is not alone when its ill effects are felt. To dream of a tear gas attack **as one walks or takes a quiet drink with friends** indicates a yielding of power to that of another.
	If the attack comes when **one is with one's family**, the dream predicts despondency.
Teasmade	Home transformed.
Techno Music	A string of relationships to come, each less satisfying than the last.
Teflon	Thanks to the last minute intervention of a friend you will make light work of a heavy load.
Tekken	Sleep loss; red-eye flights; conflict in offices, playgrounds or gardens.

Telephone Ringing but You Can't Find It
Lost chances, erasures, missed opportunities.

Telephone Ringing from a Callbox in the Street
This dream means that you will shortly have an encounter with a stranger.

Telephone Romance
The romance begins, prospers and ends without a single real meeting. One of the parties might be someone who works in telesales or as a personal assistant, or just someone who keeps calling wrong numbers. The dream is of a love that grows through words and silences. The dream denotes purity, high standards, the importance of ideals.

Telethon To dream that you are performing in a telethon or other marathon charity event is a premonition of difficult times ahead.

If the event is **some celebrity-encrusted Live Aid style thing** with everyone doing cover versions of one another's songs the hardships will be made bearable by support from family and friends.

To dream of participating in a **Sexathon** for charity, sponsored for the number of lovers or blowjobs one can get through is a dream of fidelity and great happiness.

Television To dream of watching television symbolises blindness to problems at home or work.

If the television **has bad reception** the dreamer will fail in his or her most cherished endeavours.

A dream of a television that is **leaking water** predicts inconsequential success.

To dream of a television **thrown from a tenth storey window** is a good omen and means that the social life of the dreamer will considerably improve.

To dream of being **struck by a falling television** is not so auspicious a sign, foretelling of crises arising from panic, confusion or absentmindedness.

A dream of **a room lit only by the light of a television** is a warning against intimacy with strangers, whilst a dream of **an impoverished, damp room which is furnished with only a couch and a television** foretells of wealth in the future.
See also **Watching TV Naked**

Temporary Landlord Brought in to Try to Reverse the Fortunes of an Ailing Pub A dream of a temporary landlord predicts substantial changes in the dreamer's life, the direction of the changes depending on the landlord himself.

If the dreamed landlord is **young, cheery and inexperienced** the changes will be for the worse.

If he is **old, sullen and battle-scarred** the changes will be for the better.

218

Temporary Tattoo

A temporary tattoo denotes that your heart is more changeable than you have previously dared to admit.

If the temporary tattoo is **an identification number like those worn by prisoners in the death camps** you will shortly undertake an unplanned journey by train. (*See also* **Packed Like Cattle on a Crowded Train**)

If the temporary tattoo bears **some catchphrase** or **modern slogan** the dream foretells insincerity or an outright lie.

Testcard

To dream of the **testcard** or **closedown on TV** denotes a death in the family.

Texture Dreams

Of all the strange occurrences, events, objects and spectacles in nature's fantastic cinema of sleep, the texture dream is the hardest to correctly interpret. Without narrative, location, dialogue, sound or characters, such dreams rely entirely on the production of a feeling of some substance or fluid close to and enveloping the dreamer. The Modern world, with its endless innovation in manufacturing and production processes and its endless demands for new substances, has produced a myriad of entirely new texture dreams, each of which has its own unique meaning.

As a general rule the **hot, smooth, silky or sticky** texture dreams are the optimistic ones whilst the **sharp, pin-pricking or abrasive** ones foretell darker futures.

To dream that one is **drowning in a sea of sickly smooth vinyl** predicts a marriage in the not-too-distant future, whilst a dream that one is **bathing deeply in some substance like the glutinous cleansing product Swarfega** predicts a painful divorce.

If one finds oneself **smothered by an abrasive and undulating texture like that of brushed aluminium,** a career change is on the cards.

219

If the dream involves **blind immersion in something with the texture and sickening warmth of crunchy peanut butter** the dream foresees a maritime adventure; whilst to feel that one's skin is **wrapped, folded and swathed in a texture between that of nylon and polyester** foretells illness, a change in career or the revelation of a secret by mail.

See also **Formica**

Thalidomide   Fidelity and love.

Themed Hotel   Fame, false memories, wealth.

Themed Pub   A pantomime of emotions, rejection in half-light, darkness during daytime.

See also **Irish Theme Pub**

Think Tank   Deception, subterfuge.

3D Glasses   Perverted aspirations, wealth grown by wise investments.

Tickertape Parade

Good luck and surprises on a shopping trip.

Tied at the Waist with Elasticated Rope, in a Room where the Floor is Covered in Grease or in Oil like on some Dumb Novelty Sports Contest

No matter how hard the dreamer tries to move or escape the combined efforts of rope and slippery floor always ensure that he or she is pulled back to base. The dream (which features bruised knees and brutal exhaustion) foretells of a confrontation with a parent or sibling.

See also **Running Up the Down Escalator** *and* **Urban Gridlock**

Time   There are numerous common yet characteristically Modern Dreams involving the so-called fourth dimension of time.

From the **assembly line** to the drug **Crack Cocaine** the pace and inventions of the developing world have caused many disruptions and reinventions of the human experience of time, and the cumulative consequences of this have been visited with regular abandon on the psyche of the Modern Dreamer.

Central to many of such dreams is the notion that time itself has been altered in some fundamental way. To dream that **time has been decimalised** is a warning of the dreamer's desire for order or control. If the dreamer **loses his or her own birthday** in the changes, the dream also foretells an anxious meeting with a parent or a law suit involving offspring.

To dream that time itself **has been bought or sponsored by a large corporation** is also common enough, with the major watch manufacturers like Timex, Accurist and Swatch featuring high in the roster of speculative sponsors or purchasers. This dream of the sponsorship of time signifies an unease with some aspect of the dreamer's work life or home routine. If the putative sponsors for time **are companies not normally associated with watches or time-keeping** then the meaning of the dream shifts profoundly. To dream that time has **been bought or sponsored by the drug company Hoffman/La Roche/Sandoz** or by the **style company Diesel** is a sign that unexpected changes will soon happen in the dreamer's life.

A dream that **time has been taken under state control**, its progress, measurement and affairs managed by a phalanx of greying civil servants from desks and laboratories in some bomb-proof concrete bunker of a building, is a dream with ambiguous potential. For the rich it bodes well, promising delights in food, travel and the enjoyment of culture. For the poor it predicts starvation, loss of memory and eventual mental illness.

A further genre of time-related dreams is that in which one believes that one has **invented or discovered new kinds or categories of time**. To dream of **blue** time (when one is sad or cold) is a

221

dream that predicts a shopping trip, a house-warming party or a fishing trip. To dream of **black** time (when one is confused or downhearted) is a prediction of long nights ahead, spent trying to solve some persistent and complicated problem. A dream of **soft** time (when events are more changeable or malleable than at other times) is a dream of the opposite – one will encounter nothing but stubbornness and intransigence in its wake.

No entry on the occurrence of time in Modern Dreams would be complete without comment on those frequent dreams involving **Time Travel**. Perhaps the simplest and most well-known of these is the dream in which the dreamer finds him or herself in the waiting room of some anonymous institution, **staring at an old circular analogue clock, the second hand of which is methodically making its way backwards around its face.** The dream foretells of a revival of an old love affair or an abandoned business deal; or, if the clock has luminous numerals, it foretells of the reintroduction of some antique form of transport or communication (e.g. trams). More disturbing is the dream that one is travelling much greater distances back in time, revisiting the scenes of one's youth, marriage or divorce. The meaning of this dream lies in the method of travel. If time travel is achieved **by a machine like those commonly seen in cheap television programmes** (flashing lights, plexiglass booths, perspex seating, grandiose arcs of electricity cables etc.), the dream advises caution in a purchase or timidity when giving opinions. If **the dreamer moves through time without mechanical aid** – simply arriving at some moment in the past as easily as one might visit another room in one's house – the dream foretells fortune on a game show, lottery or other game of chance.

Most peculiar and persistent of all the Modern Dreams involving time travel is that of **dealing drugs from the future to clients in the past.** This dream, with its obvious potential for scenes of paradox, absurdity and chaos (painters in sixteenth-century Japan 'turned on' to L.S.D., everyone in the eighteenth century addicted to crack etc.) is a warning that must not be ignored – the dreamer must remember to keep both a tidy house and a tidy mind in the weeks and months ahead.

Modern Dreams of **time travel to the future** are decidedly less common, for reasons which many have hotly debated and none have coolly proven. Such dreams, on those rare occasions when they do occur, are symbols of that vague unaccountable yearning which haunts the century in which we dwell – a lack, profound and inexplicable, which will never find answer on this earth.

Tinned Mince

To dream of tinned mince is a sign of poverty ahead.

If the mince is **grey** in colour the poverty may well be severe.

Toga Party

Troubles arising from the depths of the past.

If **those attending the party are naked beneath their make-shift togas** the dream portends the unmasking of some trivial deceit.

To dream of **a nylon or polyester toga** foretells of cheap gifts from a once-respected friend.

Too Close at a Cashpoint or ATM Machine

A dream in which someone stands too close behind you at a cashpoint or ATM machine indicates future uncertainty, most often in the realm of love.

There are many common Modern Dreams involving invasions of personal space and consequent discomfort, all of them unlucky. A dream of **eye contact with a fellow motorist whilst stopping for a red light** foretells especial upheaval, whilst a dream of **an overcrowded elevator** always spells misfortune in financial affairs. The worst dream of this kind is to fancy that **whilst bracing oneself on the hanging-strap of an underground**

223

train as it comes to a halt, one touches the hand of another passenger. Few people are happy in the weeks and months which follow this dream.

Topless Dancing Many Modern Dreams involve topless dancing, pole dancing, wall dancing and other derivatives. Common to all is the experience of looking but not touching. Like the dream of **handling nuclear fuel rods remotely through the agency of telematic arms (the rods contained in a sealed glass case)**, the sight of the object of one's desire combined with its untouchability is a highly potent combination, with heady results in the kingdom of sleep.

Topless dancing, pole dancing, wall dancing and go-go dancing all signify political impotence and lack of influence. For the man seeking custody of his children it means failure; for the small shop-holder seeking a license for an extension of business hours it means certain rejection; for the common man seeking favours from a king, a city council or a Justice of the Peace it means a negative decision, no matter how strong the case.

See also **Podium Dancers**

Tourists Request that You Take their Photograph

If the tourists are **Japanese** the dream is bad luck.

If they are **Italian** it is very bad luck.

If **it is hard to understand how to work the camera** the meaning of the dream is reversed.

A dream in which **the tourists set an impossible task** (e.g.: get both of us and the whole of the Eiffel Tower into the picture) is a sign of a future triumph.

Trading Cards Insecurity in a business venture, inhospitality in a hotel, hostel or bed-and-breakfast, ingratitude in a child.

Training Shoe on Top of a Bus Shelter

If the shoe is a **Reebok** the dream foretells of success in the garden or in homemaking.

224

If the shoe is an **Adidas** it foretells of success in one's travel plans.

If the shoe is a **Nike** it foretells of good luck in romance.

Only **a blue sneaker/plimsoll** on top of a bus shelter foretells of ill fortune, predicting despair and the prospect of suicide.

However in any of these instances if the training shoe is **rotten** the meaning of the dream is reversed.

Transporter Room

To dream of the transporter room from the famous television series *Star Trek* predicts substantial alterations to one's house or garden.

A dream in which one is actually transported depends for its meaning on the feeling experienced as one dissolves or rematerialises. A **giddy** feeling predicts a romance, a **numb** feeling predicts a death.

See also **James T. Kirk/William Shatner**

Travelator   Promotion.

Trees Planted after the Riots

A dream of the bitter and miserable saplings planted in the worst housing estates of England after the riots in the 1980s predicts a fall from grace, an act of repentance or a journey to visit friends.

Trench Warfare   The excesses and advances of Modern warfare have left their scars deep on the psychic flesh of our times, especially in regard to the cramped conditions of the trenches. The dream of trench warfare, up to one's knees or waist in mud, living on scraps, surrounded by the dead, enveloped in cold and constantly fearing attack is a dream of ambiguous feelings towards one's family.

If **one's comrades in the trench are dying** the family will survive, if **one's comrades are already dead** a rift will rend one's home asunder.

Similar in tone and meaning (but different in

setting) is the dream of **High Rise Living,** in which the dreamer strives to survive in a cramped and decaying living space, impossibly crowded with children, toddlers, babies, teenagers, unemployed adults and assorted uncles. **If music can be heard from the other side of the paper-thin walls and floors** the dream predicts a marriage, a party or a wake. **If shouting, weeping or yelling can be heard** the dream predicts a fight.

Trial by Juke Box Jury

To dream that one's fate, and the execution of justice, lies in the hands of a small team of minor celebrities foretells a time of despair and disillusion. For the gardener there will be weeds, for the schoolteacher accusations of violence and molestation, and for the postman angry, hungry and unchained dogs along the route.

If any of the celebrities are wearing glasses with 'zany' frames or ties with supposedly humorous designs the despair and disillusion will be but short-lived.

Trial Separation   The dream predicts a business merger.

If there is acrimony and dispute over who should move out, or over how long the 'trial' itself should last there is good profit to be made in the merger.

Trivia Quiz   You will have to care for children, some yours and others belonging to friends.

Trying to Locate Someone Using a Mobile Phone

Arriving to meet a friend at a railway station, crowded street or in some vast public building, the dreamer searches but is unable to locate them. After a time the dreamer calls from a mobile to that of the person he or she seeks and it soon transpires that each party is somewhere in the same location, even though they cannot see each other. Descriptions of precise locations in the station, street or building are exchanged – by the exit from a subway, near the stairwell at the front or back, by

226

the fountain or by the Burger King – often to no avail, since dream stations have a collection of such landmarks, many of them identical. The task of finding each other can go on for ages, the mobile commentary providing both clues and a preposterous hindrance to the dreamer's endeavours. The dream speaks of grand ambitions thwarted.

If people in the dream are **staring** as the dreamer searches, gives commentary on his or her location and then searches again, the dream predicts an unexpected climb to fame.

Trying, Without Success, to Get the Volume of the TV Just Right

A dream in which no amount of adjustment to the volume can alter the fact that when it is set with one notch on the on-screen display the volume is too quiet and when set with two notches it is way too loud. The dream predicts hesitation that will prove costly.

Related are the dreams of **endlessly tweaking the heat control of the shower in an attempt to get the temperature right** and that of **wandering around the room with a TV aerial in one's hands, raising and lowering it repeatedly, in a vain attempt to get a good picture.** The former predicts a volatile family situation, the latter a misunderstanding caused by hasty judgement or poor communication.

Tupperware Party

A young woman telephones her friends, work colleagues and acquaintances and invites them to come to her house that evening to sample in full the range of products created by a leading manufacturer of home storage products ... the dream of a Tupperware party has often been followed by unhappiness and suicide.

Turf War
A warning against making promises you cannot keep.

Turlington, Christy
You will be happy.

TV	*See* Television
TV Chef	Sexual desire.
TV Newsroom	If the newsroom is in a state of high energy panic, hysterical as some news story breaks, the dreamer will enjoy a pleasurable vacation.
	If the newsroom is **deserted** the dreamer will suffer setbacks in love.

U

U.F.Os

If the U.F.Os are **in the sky**, appearing as blurred lights, streaks of fire, spinning circles and patterns of dots, the dream predicts encounters with strangers, with new information and with unexpected doubts.

If the U.F.Os have landed, doors open, ramps deployed, the dream is of moving house, of runaway children or of lost innocence.

Unable to Urinate

See **Silence at the Urinal**

Underclass

To dream of an underclass is to see your own secrets clearly, without the filters of fantasy or pride.

If the underclass is **sullen, silent or brooding** the dream is of your secrets faced with remorse.

If the dream is of an underclass **at play (dancing, revelling, drug-taking, gambling)** your secrets can be considered and accepted with joy.

Underpass

Modern life is full of artificial subterranea which function as conduits for journeys long and short. Whether they be underpasses, railway tunnels, the networks of subways or systems of platforms, walkways and tunnels for our many underground trains, the dream of any of these denotes struggle. An expected birth will be difficult (breach or caesarean), a project in writing will be arduous (incoherent, late for its deadline), a holiday will turn sour (constant drilling in the foundations next door, an outbreak of cramps or diarrhoea).

Worst of all is the dream of **travelling on foot in the darkness along the narrow tracks of the**

Channel Tunnel. Those who dream this dream face certain illness, often prolonged.

Underwater Action Sequence

The dream contains blurred faces, hand to hand struggles, air bubbles, deep blues and shimmering greens. It is a sentimental dream predicting saccharine pleasure.

Unfamiliar or Nonsensical Road Sign

Those who are engaged in seeking wealth will find it very quickly.

Unisex Changing Facility

Ambiguous feelings for a friend; a crossroads of decisions which must be faced with strength.

Unisex Clothing

Suspicions, blunt words, unattributed whisperings.

Unisex Hair Salon

Irregularities in paperwork; divisions in a family, business or state.

Unknown Electrical Goods

The dream involves a purchase from some warehouse or out-of-town discount store. The goods may be 'like' some everyday appliance but are different in some vague and unknowable way.

In other versions of the dream the goods are a cross between two or more perfectly common items, so that the dreamer finds him or herself purchasing a hybrid or misshapen microwave which is somehow at the same time an electrical toothbrush and a food blender. Such dreams predict unresolvable conflicts and stresses between different areas of responsibility in the dreamer's life. If the item **does not function** the conflict will be physical.

In a common variation of the dream an item of **fixed and clear function is purchased**, be it teasmade or vacuum cleaner, only for the dreamer to discover, once 'at home' or 'on the way home' that the item has transformed, become mutant, distorted or even quite useless. This dream predicts a reversal of fortune, the end of a friendship or the passage of a child into adulthood.

See also **Negative Objects** *and* **Joined Objects**

Unmarked Vehicles

A dream of deception, hatred masquerading as friendship, crooked dealings in business, false intentions in love.

If the vehicles have **tinted glass** the dreamer him or herself will be the perpetrator of dishonesty and subterfuge.

Unofficial or Bootleg Tour Merchandise
Integrity, honesty, true love.

Unpaid Electricity Bills

Riches by post, ambiguous atmospheres, blood relations at the door.

Urban Gridlock
The dreamer soars high above a city in which every street, freeway and exit ramp is solid with motionless vehicles, their drivers bored and frustrated, listening to the radio and making mobile phone calls. The dream predicts a difficult meeting with an old enemy, long forgotten.

If the **radio of a car in such gridlock plays three love songs back-to-back** in the dream the meeting predicted will be with an old friend.

If **the trapped drivers get angry, leaving their cars or blowing their horns** the dream changes its meaning entirely – there will soon be a need for new purchases in the dreamer's home or that of a friend.

See also **Running Up the Down Escalator** *and* **Tied at the Waist with Elasticated Tape**

Urine Test
Degradation, dishonour, mistrust.

If the dream is of **urinating into a whisky bottle or jam jar** the strength of its meaning is doubled.

To dream that **someone watches you as you try to give a sample for a urine test** means that the eyes of your colleagues will be on you in the weeks and months ahead.

231

A dream in which you are purchasing clean urine in order to get successfully through a test predicts honesty from colleagues and friends. If the purchased urine is a strange or unexpected colour the meaning of the dream is reversed.

Used or Soiled Underwear in the Post

The meaning of the dream depends on the roles the used or soiled underwear plays and the reasons for it being in the post.

If the dreamer is sending used underwear through the post to excite or titillate a lover the dream foretells that a confusion of identity, or a mix-up about names is in the offing.

If the dreamer is posting used or soiled underwear on a professional basis (as part of a dubious or immoral business venture) the dream augurs ill for true love.

To receive used underwear depends for its meaning on the persons involved and the reasons for its presence. If the underwear comes from a lover the dream foretells of a conflict, possibly ending in violence. If the underwear has been purchased by the dreamer it augurs well for true love. If used or soiled underwear is sent by a stranger the dream predicts an intrigue involving a close friend.

V

Vacant Lot   Pleasure, wealth, fulfilment, prosperity.

Vaginal Deodorant

The most spurious consumer product on earth foretells an accident when it appears in a dream.
See also **I Can't Believe It's Not Butter**

Valium   Lovesickness in the strong; erasure of memory; silence in a phone call.

VCR   Faced with a thick manual translated from Korean through Spanish to French via German and thence to English you **struggle to programme the VCR**, pressing buttons, considering diagrams, entering alphanumeric codes and swearing repeatedly.

If **the programme records** your actions in a forthcoming crisis will enhance your reputation.

If **it does not** you will have to defend your reputation against malicious gossip.

Vegeburger   Bad tempers, twisted arguments.

If the 'burger' is **more a mush of soft vegetables held together in a stiff cheese slop and covered in breadcrumbs** the dream is one predicting a sudden reversal of fortunes.

Velcro Fastenings   The clever fastening material Velcro is a symbol of community loyalty when it appears in a dream.

Vending Machine   Your goals are mistaken, the means chosen to achieve them false.

A dream of **a vending machine which has been vandalised** betokens strength and persistence in a time of crisis.

233

Venetian Blind Light split in slithers by a Venetian blind, casting strips of brilliant sunshine onto the opposite wall or casting rectilinear shadows onto a face stands for forthcoming mystery and intrigue, favourable for women and destructive for men.

Ventolin Inhaler A dream of a Ventolin inhaler, with a grey plastic holder and white cylinder of pressurised medicinal gas, predicts a period of greater reliance on others.

If the Ventolin has been **stolen by a malicious ex-lover** the dream foretells stability, inheritance, good fortunes.

Viagra (Black Market)

The dream of the search for black market Viagra involves an internet 'doctor' and a long wait for a plainly-wrapped parcel. It is the long wait which characterises this dream and, like the eerie feeling produced in the common dream of **an air-bag which fails to inflate,** it hangs on a sense of expectation which is somehow never to be resolved. Though far from catastrophic in their effect the dreamers of these dreams are rarely contented in the days which follow them.

Vibrator Strength, persistence, agreement marred by compromise.

Video Games A week of time slowed, phone calls at night, blurred memories of friends and former lovers cause distress and unhappiness.

Video Wall To see your own image on a video wall is to dream of confusion, split loyalties and dubious motives. The more TVs across which the dreamer's image is split the more confusion there will be.

Viper Rooms The notorious Los Angeles night-club-cum-celebrity-hang-out, the Viper Rooms, is a bad omen in a dream, auguring ill for the dreamer and all future plans.

Virtual Dongle The dreamer will all too easily compromise.

Virus   A **computer virus** stands for physical illness, deep and long-lasting, when it appears in a dream.

VISA Card will Not Swipe

Hesitations at the altar; invective in the bedroom; disorder in the street; dangerous misreadings of the small print.

See also **Coins Rejected by a Pay & Display Machine, Currency Changes, Chocolate Money** *and* **Money Stolen or Eaten by a Vending Machine**

Vomit Trails in the Neighbourhood of a Night Club or Take-Away

To dream of a trail of vomit, each pool or splash identical in its constituency but increasing in size as the path moves from litter-bin to doorway to bench to wheel arch to paving slab, in the vicinity of a nightclub, chip shop or curry house, predicts trouble with the law, a visit from old friends or a demand from a stranger to tell a story.

If the trail of vomit is **decreasing in size** the dream stands for loss of reputation, illness and diminished potency.

If the trail is one of **blood**, splatters and red raindrops making a pathway through the city streets, the dream foretells of euphoria, happiness, new life.

W

Waiting at a Traffic Light which you soon Suspect is Stuck on Red
Anxiety in the boardroom, pleasure in the bedroom.

Waking in a Stranger's Bed
If the stranger is **sleeping beside you** the dream predicts a romance.

If the stranger has **gone** the dream predicts a divorce.

Walking on Shattered Windscreen Glass
Reminders in the post, warnings by telephone and secrets told by whispering.

Walkman
Loneliness comes to those who dream of the popular miniaturised personal stereo system.

A dream of **being present at a family occasion whilst wearing a Walkman** foretells of a difference of opinion leading to a fight, whilst the common sexual dream in which one is **going down** on a **partner whilst listening to music on a Walkman** augurs ill for those intending marriage or expecting promotion.

A dream of wearing a Walkman **whilst walking the streets of a city at night** is a melodramatic dream whose meaning lies in the amount of irony involved. If one is **serious** the dream foretells unhappiness. If one is **ironic** or **playful, walking in the dark streets and smiling at the absurdity of it all**, the dream foretells success in plans, good luck in gambling and good sport in bed.

Wallpaper
To dream of **stripping** wallpaper is a dream of forgetting or of healing from some psychic or emotional wound. The longer it takes the longer the limbo of recovery will continue. If the

237

removing of the wallpaper **reveals more and more layers underneath,** the dream predicts a spell in therapy or counselling.

War Crimes Tribunal at The Hague
An argument must be settled with the help of a friend.

Warhol, Andy
You will be famous.

Warm-Up Act
To dream that you are onstage as part of a warm-up act or support act is a dream of its opposite. You will have great fame.

If the crowd is lukewarm or disinterested your fame will be matched by contentment.

Washing-Up Gloves
There will be bloody or violent work ahead.

Washing-Up Liquid
Sex in the daytime, hardship by night.

Watching the Big Day Again on Video
A dream of watching your wedding day again on video is a dream of impending loss. Money will be squandered or stolen, a special chance or moment will have gone before it is noticed, a meaning will slip through your fingers as all sit powerless to act.

If the wedding video **has a lot of boring God-stuff from the fucking vicar on it** the dream foretells a long dark night in accident and emergency.

If the VHS **shows scenes from the knees-up afterwards,** with all the lads doing the can-can and someone getting off with one of the bridesmaids the dream predicts divorce.

If **the tape is distorted in sound or picture,** or if there are **unexplained gaps** in it, you will suffer drink problems or difficulties with unruly children.

Watching TV from a Safe Position Hidden Behind the Sofa
The meaning of this dream depends on the programme being watched.

If it is a **horror film** you will find true love.

If it is a **kids' program**me you will have many children.

If it is the **news** you will die alone.

Watching TV Naked
You are about to enter a vulnerable period in your life.

See also **Television**

Watergate Tapes
To dream of the Watergate tapes is to dream that your own efforts will undo you. Just as the paranoid and mistrustful President Nixon was caught lying by his own surveillance equipment, so too will you be trapped by plans or actions meant to further your own goals.

A related dream is that of **finding the Watergate tapes amongst a pile of junk at a car-boot sale** – like other classic Modern Dreams (such as finding a **diary kept by Hitler amongst a box of old papers in the attic**) the meaning lies most in its revelation of the malleability of evidence and, by implication, the past itself. You should feel both confident that bad times in recent days, weeks or months will soon be forgotten and wary that the truth will one day emerge.

Wave Machine
Emotional troubles, outbursts, unexpected distress.

Wearing a Wire
A bitter, anxious dream of betrayal which stands most often for a crossroads in your life; a warning to cut your losses, put yourself first and get out on top.

If the wire gets **seen** you will prosper in haulage or industry.

If **the tape leaves a mark or red patch on the skin when removed** your secrets will be stolen by an intimate friend.

If the wire **fails to work** (power loss, disturbance on the frequency, loose connections) the dream foretells of an accident involving cars or cooking implements.

The acts of **confessing to love** or of **having sexual**

intercourse whilst wearing a wire have the same meaning in a dream – those with secrets will be found out, those with pride will have it wounded.

Weeping at the Checkout

Love – deep, true and long-lasting – comes to he or she who dreams of weeping at a supermarket checkout.

Weeping on a Gameshow

There will be a chance for change and the dreamer must take it.

Weeping on the Telephone

Failure in business.

'Welcome' Doormat Cut in Half

You will be loved but that will not be enough.

Wet T-shirt Competition

If you are a **contestant** the dream augurs well for future plans.

If you are a **judge** you will lose status in the eyes of a friend.

Wheel Clamping You will incur the displeasure of a companion.

White Flight The process by which rich white people flee the inner cities, abandoning them to the poor and racial minorities stands for shame, wealth and the abuse of power in a dream.

White People Using the word 'Nigger'

A warning about a marriage, friendship or contract about to be entered into.

White Teeth A dream of the Colgate smile ©, perfect teeth gleaming a vivid and limitless white, predicts great loss and displeasure incurred in strife.

Whoopee Cushion

Stark truth regarding friends and enemies.

If the cushion is of **the Johnny Fart Pants brand** your old age will be marred by illness.

Wife and Children Replaced by Robots

This common dream signifies the dreamer's unease with his life.

See also **Stunt Man**

Wife-Beating Promotion at work.

Wife Swapping Chance encounters, mistakes in darkness.

See also **Key Party**

Window Box If its contents **flower**, a dream of a window box is an omen of domestic strife.

If its contents **wither and die** the meaning of the dream is reversed.

Window Shopping

Great restlessness, discomfort and dissatisfaction will come to he or she who dreams of window shopping.

Winos The distinctive urban hobos known variously as winos, dossers and cider-boys are frequent figures in the cityscapes of Modern Dreams. Never far from a Safeway, an underpass or a bus station these stinking specimens, whilst outside of society at large, are powerful symbols for the dreamer's social and other status.

A dream of winos **sitting harmlessly on a bench in the sun and enjoying their cider** is a dream of marital bliss and harmony.

If the winos are **querulous, yelling at each other or at passersby** the dreamer's marriage will be troubled and tempestuous.

A dream of winos who are **crazy** – directing imaginary traffic, barking like dogs or negotiating vivid deals with invisible spirits or ghosts in the air around them – predicts success in the world of politics and public affairs.

To dream of **kissing a wino** (the taste of decay crossed with Special Brew, ketchup, burger and nicotine) is a dream of death, whilst to dream of **making love** to a wino (hurried action in the bushes of the Peace Garden, or a blow job behind the skips

241

at the back of Debenhams) predicts recovery from illness, repayment of debt or re-entry to a pub from which the dreamer has been barred.

Wire Fu
The genre of Kung Fu movies in which you can see that the actors are being supported by wires as they jump, kick, leap and sail through the air is a symbol of strength in an important friendship in a dream.

If the wired-up fighters are **women** your friendship could turn into a romance.

Witness Protection Programme
To dream of entering the witness protection programme means that you must make adjustments to your character or behaviour at home or at work.

To dream of **a loved one entering the witness protection programme** means that they are false and will desert you.

Woman Coming Down the Concourse of a Heathrow Terminal, Deeply Engrossed in a Private Conversation on a Hands-Free Mobile Kit, Her Eyes Focused Elsewhere, Her Gestures and Her Smiles so very Intimate that You Cannot Believe that the Person she is Talking to is not Actually There
A dream predicting amazement, astonishment and a surprise which borders on the sublime.

Woman who is Not Over her Previous Relationship
To dream of a woman who is not over her previous relationship is a good omen.

If she is **crying** it is a very good omen, especially for those involved in the medical profession.

If she **cries during sexual intercourse** the meaning of the dream is reversed.

Working for £2.40 per hour
The Modern Dreamer is used to such dreams in which the value of his or her labour is estimated at below the legal minimum. The exact meaning of these shaming dreams depends on the nature of the work.

If it is **assembling biros** the dream foretells of the arrival of a letter.

If it is **telesales** the dreamer will be kissed by a handsome stranger.

If the work is unusual, like **solving strange riddles** or **trying to contact the dead for a research programme** or **doing crosswords and anagrams,** the dream foretells of great loss, or great sadness with unexpected cause.

Working on the Nightshift at the Birds' Trifle Factory in Paignton

A common dream in which the happiness predicted rises in direct proportion to productivity in the factory.

If the labourforce is **dedicated and hardworking** the dreamer will prosper.

If the workforce is **slovenly, prone to bouts of illegal sleeping and excessive tea-breaks,** the dreamer's future happiness will be that much the less.

The dream takes on a special meaning if the factory is **dogged by mechanical or electrical failure** – conveyor belts jamming, lights flickering, food pipes getting blocked etc. In such cases an unexpected change of address is predicted.

If the dream involves a **food fight using ingredients from the trifle mixture** there will be bad news arriving by airmail or telephone.

Work to Rule   Breakdown in a marriage, trouble in a pub, restaurant or bar.

Works Canteen   Unrequited love.

Wounded by a Frisbee

The most trusted of your friends is a traitor.

Wrap Party   A bad omen predicting strife, compromise and business embarrassment.

Wreckage of a 747, Strewn over many Miles

The dreamer walks or drives through a landscape in which the trees, pylons, gardens and rooftops are covered with the strange snowfall of a thousand or more shattered suitcases. Here and there on the

243

pavements and lawns are shoes, paperback books, night-gowns, towels, swimming suits, coats, thongs, digital clocks, exploded bottles of Ambre Solaire. The dream is of new friends found in sudden intimacy through work or hardship.

If the dreamer finds a **wallet** in the wreckage the dream is of great fortune.

To find **a sole survivor**, wandering from the crash scene in a state of shock, is a dream of loneliness to come.

To hear a **phone or pager ringing** in the wreckage is a reminder of some long-neglected duty.

Wrong Numbers A dream of dialling a wrong number **yourself** means that a chance encounter will take place in your life.

To dream that you **receive** a wrong-number call is to anticipate a death, or illness, possibly your own.

X

Xanax The powerful prescription 'happy pill' stands for hope against the odds if taken in a dream.

X-Ray Glasses Deception.

X-Ray of a Skull Following the dream you should learn to trust your insights and perceptions.

X-Rated Movies Love begun and ended by night.
See also **Censored Film**

Y

Yakuza The Japanese organised crime syndicate stands for loyalty, fierceness, refusal to retreat when seen in a dream.

Yardies These formidable Jamaican gangsters are known internationally as purveyors of organised crime. In a dream they have a different function, namely as agents who bind together different symbols.

Alone, a Yardie has no meaning in a dream, but if he **steals a watch from one person and gives it to another** he connects the protagonists of many Modern Dreams.

A Yardie may connect objects with people, people with people, objects with places, places with places. Indeed many dreams of a Yardie may be interpreted by a careful analysis of his route as he struts through the streets of a city.

A Yardie **who meets no people, walks no streets and handles no objects (stolen or not)** has no meaning in a dream.

See also **Geeks** *and* **Rastafarian**

You Live Your Whole Life in a Place and Never Taste the Thing That it's Famous For A dream of unhappiness which comes and goes for no reason.

Youth Club A dream of a youth club predicts happiness in old age.

If there are **boys smoking in the toilets** the dream is of truths disappearing.

Youth Cults *See* **Gothic Punks, Grebos, Hell's Angels** *and* **Skinheads**

Z

Zapping   *See* **Channel Hopping**

Zapruder Dream (or Home Movie Has Unwittingly Captured a
Historical Event)   Ever since Zapruder shot his unfortunate and
                         unintentional record of the Kennedy Assassination
                         (21 August 1962) this dream has been known by
                         his name. Whether involving a sea-side home
                         movie with a background of a ship going down, or
                         a children's birthday picnic with a viscous political
                         murder in the background, the Zapruder dream in
                         all its many forms predicts a strange and
                         unexpected correlation between your own life and
                         that of a stranger. It may be that a stranger
                         encountered on a bus will leave you a fortune, or
                         that a whispered word from a person unknown to
                         you will change the whole direction of your life,
                         but you can be assured that following the Zapruder
                         dream life will change, as a most unpredictable
                         connection is made.
                         See also **Death Has Been Unwittingly Captured**
                         On Amateur Video

Zebra Crossing   A dream of new possibilities, daydreams realised,
                         pathways appearing through dilemmas long
                         thought insoluble.

Zeppelin Raids   To dream of these great airships dropping bombs,
                         raining death and destruction on the cities below, is
                         a dream of peace. The greater the destruction the
                         more perfect the contentment predicted.

Zero Gravity   To dream of zero gravity means that you will have
                         an argument with someone who is lighter than you.
                         See also **Sex Experiments in Space**

Zip	To dream of a **Zip** or of **Zippers** predicts sharp words from a close friend.
	A dream in which you are **wearing clothes which seem to have too many zips** foretells of misfortune in the financial markets.
Zimmer Frame	A dream of inarticulacy. Arguments will be lost, explanations bungled, stories told badly or left incomplete.
Zoned Out	The dreamer is being warned to skip work conflict whenever possible – take the short route, the low road and the path of least resistance.

Zoo Animals at Large in the City

Elephants on the rampage in a shopping mall, giraffes grazing in the city park, lions loose in a multi-storey car park all signify a time of great change.

Zoom Lens	A dream of **looking through a zoom lens** is a warning to mind your own business, whilst a dream in which **you are being observed with the aid of a zoom lens** is a warning of about a neighbour who is up to no good.
Z.Z. Top	A dream of the quirky bearded rockers denotes a mystery which cannot be solved.